Charles Costesworth Beaman

A Historical Address

Delivered in Scituate, Rhode Island

Charles Costesworth Beaman

A Historical Address
Delivered in Scituate, Rhode Island

ISBN/EAN: 9783744733878

Printed in Europe, USA, Canada, Australia, Japan

Cover: Foto ©ninafisch / pixelio.de

More available books at **www.hansebooks.com**

AN

HISTORICAL ADDRESS,

DELIVERED IN

SCITUATE, RHODE ISLAND,

July 4th, 1876,

AT THE REQUEST OF THE TOWN AUTHORITIES,

BY C. C. BEAMAN.

PHENIX:
CAPRON & CAMPBELL, STEAM BOOK AND JOB PRINTERS.
1877.

THE OCCASION.

The great republic of the world celebrates its first century to-day! It has invited all nations to participate in the occasion by an exhibition of the products and workmanship of their respective countries, in the city where the assembled Congress framed, adopted, and sent forth, July Fourth, 1776, their Declaration of Independence. It has selected an orator and poet, and other exercises appropriate to the event to take place in the same city. Our own State has requested, through its legislature, that every town in our borders should have a local celebration; and Congress and the President have sent a similar appeal to every town in the Union.

The extraordinary growth of the country in the last century, the very high position it occupies to-day, the success on so large a scale, and for so long a period, of a free government, would seem to demand an uncommon manifestation of the nation, on the happy event of completing our first one hundred years; and that to-day our Union is perfect and complete, with not a single star blotted out from our banner, and many more added to the original thirteen, standing to-day stronger and more immovable than ever.

It was with fear and trembling, one hundred years ago, that the delegates from the colonies assembled in a small hall in Philadelphia, put forth their immortal Declaration, July 4, 1776. They were wise and prudent men—some of them, as was our own Hopkins, advanced in years; a few, like Hancock, were rich. They all had much at stake, having families, high character, the ablest men chosen from Virginia, Massachusetts, Rhode Island and the other

colonies : they exposed themselves, in case of defeat, to confis-
cation of property, banishment, imprisonment, loss of reputation,
and death by being hung as traitors, but they drew not back, there
was no faltering while they cut the tie which bound them to the
mother country, and launched their bark upon the tempestuous
ocean of conflict with a mighty nation that had the resources of a
standing army, vessels of war, wealth, and all the munitions ready
for instantaneous and deadly war. To oppose all this strength of
warlike array, there were a few regiments of militia, no ship of
war, and guns, cannon balls and powder; and other requisites of
military warfare were few indeed, and neither money nor credit
but in a very limited degree.

The infant Congress staggered not at the impending and
deadly struggle looming up at the future, and boldly appealed to
the arbitration of the sword, and the decision of the impartial nations of the world :

" When," they said, commencing their declaration, " in the
course of human events, it becomes necessary for one people to dis-
solve the political bonds which have connected them with another,
and to assume among the powers of the earth, the separate and
equal station to which the laws of nature and of nature's God en-
title them, a decent respect for the opinions of mankind requires
that they should declare the causes which impel them to the sepa-
ration."

Many and dear were the ties which bound them to the mother
country ! It was beyond other great nations, a free country ; and
the men of the revolution often expressed themselves as demanding
nothing more than the rights of a British subject enjoyed at home.
England was dear to them, as the source whence their supplies and
protection proceeded ; they had an interest in her glory as a nation ; as
the country from whose bosom the colonies came as from a mother.
Their literature, religion, language and customs had been brought
over to America—the graves of ancestry made the burial places of
Britain dear to Americans. Ties of interest, affection and consan-
guinity were sundered with regret.

But Great Britain, her rulers, and her people looked upon the colonies to be sources of pecuniary profit; they were jealous of all manufactures and commerce which interfered with their own ; and by custom-house taxes and vexatious laws to prevent the Americans from trading with any people but England and her colonies, they turned the love of the people into hatred.   The people were treated in some respects as a conquered or dependent race, and not to be ranked in privilege and honor with subjects at home.   All these reasons, and more, are stated in the declaration ; then comes the solemn determination that they will bear the injustice and oppression no longer, but set up for themselves.   In well considered words they take their final farewell :

" We, therefore, the representatives of the United States of America, in General Congress assembled, appealing to the Supreme Judge of the world for the rectitude of our intentions, do, in the name and by the authority of the good people of these colonies, solemnly publish and declare, that these united colonies are, and of right ought to be, free and independent states ; that they are absolved from all allegiance to the British crown, and that all political connection between them and the state of Great Britain, is, and ought to be totally dissolved :   and that as free and independent states they have full power to levy war, conclude peace, contract alliances, establish commerce, and to do all other acts and things which independent states may of right do.   And for the support of this declaration, with a firm reliance on the protection of Divine Providence, we mutually pledge to each other our lives, our fortunes and our sacred honor."

The fighting at Concord and Lexington had already taken place, and two months afterwards the battle of Bunker Hill sent its echo round the world.   Boston had been evacuated by the British forces March 17, 1776, and now, July 4, 1776, the rebellion had taken shape in an official act of the newly organized government, casting off all allegiance to Great Britain, and asserting its entire independence and determination to maintain it by all the force they could command.

We meet to-day without distinction of party or religious de-
nomination ; and though we come together as town's people of
Scituate, we hold fellowship with all the towns of our State, and
passing out of the bounds of Rhode Island we stand up to-day with
every state, city and town in the Union in a GRAND NATIONAL JUBILEE!
on the occasion of our completing our *first hundred years.* We
go farther, and extend a call to every other nation to rejoice with us
in our remarkable history; in the unexampled prosperity we have
enjoyed, in the success which has attended the experiment of a people self-governed. We may be pardoned for some little self-ex-
ultation while we recognize the guiding hand of our God in our preservation and blessing.

In the city of Philadelphia, where our delegates in Congress
assembled a hundred years ago, and framed and adopted a Declaration of Independence there will be an extraordinary gathering of
our fellow citizens from all parts of our country, and many distinguished visitors from foreign lands will be convened to witness a
national festival, commemorative of what transpired in that city a
hundred years ago, and what great results have come out of it.)

We have dared to invite an International Exhibition of Art
and Manufactures, Inventions and Discoveries, Literature and Sci-
ence, and other matters relating to man's progress in society, and
to put side by side, our own skill and taste, not for vain show, but
in order to bring the world into fellowship and useful and honorable competition.   •

/ We may not be able to grasp in our vision the spectacle which
our still youthful nation presents to the world to-day. *Our* place
is in the New World discovered by Christopher Columbus four
hundred years ago. The vast extent of territory that maps out our
heritage lying between two great oceans; its natural features of
mountains, valleys and plains, and lakes and rivers, indented coasts
by inlets, bays and harbors where proud navies ride and prosperous
cities lift their spires is but imperfectly realized. A view of the
manufacturing and mechanical establishments, a sight of the farms
cultivated with all the help of newly invented agricultural imple- ·

ments, a perception of the warehouses where are stored the productions and workmanship of every clime, the schools and colleges filled with pupils of both sexes, the churches whose bells ring cheerfully on the Sabbath morn, the printing presses worked by steam power, scattering leaves of knowledge over the whole land, the railroads running in every direction, bearing immense freights and conveying passengers in multitude, the telegraph with its wires beneath the'ocean and stretched out over the whole land, and the activity of the people, and the enterprise visible, and the arrivals of emigrants daily from the four quarters of the globe, with the general intelligence, comfort and happiness of the people, the steady march of population over the deserts, or uncultivated places, and the returning march from the West to meet midway the East; this is the picture too great and wonderful to be fully realized, as the orators of our centennary year vainly strive with uplifted voice and choice expression to describe to-day in the assemblies convened all over the land.

Praise and thanksgiving may well go up from the nation so highly favored of God! who has not so blessed every other nation under the broad heavens—no other nation has a history like ours. Behold what God has wrought for us! May thanks go up from the shores of both oceans, and from the banks of every river and lake, from every hill and valley, and all places where man has set his foot on the soil of these United States and sheltered himself from oppression and wrong beneath the folds of our star spangled banner.

Berkeley, the English philosopher, who made for a while his home in Newport, in 1730, filled as it were with superhuman foresight of the coming glory of America, wrote the well-known prophetic lines :

> " Westward the course of empire takes its way;
> The first four acts already past,
> A fifth shall close the drama with the day—
> Time's noblest offspring is the last! "

SCITUATE IN EARLY DAYS.

The arriving of a centennial year naturally turns our thoughts to the past. We revert to the beginning and progress of men and things, and love to connect old things with new. It is a duty which we owe to those who have gone before us to consider their wrongs and enquire for their principles! We cannot go back like China, Japan and India, to a very remote past, for our country is very new; but we may turn to ancient and discolored manuscripts, antiquated house furniture, old houses, by-gone burial places, deeds of valor, primitive and frugal ways, times of poverty and need, of honesty and patriotism, to the period of forest and self-denying and perilous lives, to the simple faith and child-like trust in God of the early days.

Wealth and luxury, numbers and power, things that are new and wonderful we can see every day and year, but we must make special exertion and set apart a time to explore the past and ruminate in the quiet shades of by-gone generations. We have before us to-day a *town history:* one that is eventful, that called out human strength and fortitude in an extraordinary degree, and developed what is good and noble in man and in communities.

It will be expected of me, on the present occasion, to present some outlines of the history of Scituate. Like other parts of Rhode Island, it was first inhabited by Indians, and the territory remained in a state of nature, for the red men were hunters and fishers, cultivating only little patches of ground, of corn, tobacco, beans, etc. Little collections of huts or wigwams formed their towns—of which there may have been a dozen in many miles travel.

The settlement of Roger Williams at Providence in 1636 is the commencement of our history. He dedicated himself to the spread of the gospel among the Indians, and traveled among the different tribes who were at war with each other, to pacify them and satisfy them that he and his associates had honest intentions to live peaceably with them. God gave him with Canonicus, the great and powerful Indian chief, favor so that he obtained as a gift large and valuable tracts of land. The deed of gift was dated March 24, 1637, in the second year of the Rhode Island plantation and reads —" in consideration of the many kindnesses and services he hath continually done for us." The land given was of the lands upon

Mooshansick and Woonasquatucket rivers. Soon after this grant, Mr. Williams, in an unselfish spirit, executed a deed giving an equal share with himself to twelve of his companions, and "such other as the major part of us shall admit into the same fellowship of vote with us." All of them, with others, fifty-four in all, had lots assigned them, in the first division of land, which took place soon after the initial deed was accepted.

The settlement increased, as from other colonies and from beyond the sea, emigrants continued to arrive, and numbers spread themselves over the wooded heights and vales of that part of Providence afterwards set off as Scituate.

It was formerly the practice—that is soon after the proprietors connected with Roger Williams had been increased to one hundred, that persons "took up lands," as the current phrase was, that they had them surveyed and marked off, and entered upon the records—some compensation may have been given to the proprietors. Deeds were however in early use; an old one was found not long ago, among the papers of Gideon Harris, bearing date 1661, of the size of half a sheet of letter paper, written on both sides, and with the curious orthography of the olden time.)

The first settlers of Scituate drove no large herds and flocks before them, and there were no meadows for a supply of grass to feed them; at first, probably, men alone came to build a rough cabin and make a clearing, and afterwards, they brought their families. The soil was good, but it was rocky and covered with woods. Wild beasts and Indians roved over it. Stephen Hopkins, who was born in Scituate in 1710, and lived there till middle life, in a few pages of early Rhode Island history, wrote in poetic verse the pitiable condition of the first inhabitants:

> " Nor house, nor hut, nor fruitful field,
> Nor lowing herd, nor bleating flock,
> Or garden that might comfort yield,
> Nor cheerful, early crowing cock."
>
> No orchard yielding pleasant fruit,
> Or laboring ox or useful plow;
> Nor neighing steed or browsing goat,
> Or grunting swine or feedful cow.

No friend to help, no neighbor nigh,
    Nor healing medicine to relieve;
No mother's hand to close the eye,
    Alone, forlorn, and most extremely poor."

A better class, and very enterprising and successful, came afterwards. In 1710 some emigrants arrived from Scituate, Mass. In 1730 Scituate was set off from Providence as a distinct township.

Tradition gives John Mathewson the credit of building the first white man's house—if it may be so called—in Scituate. It was a hovel or hut put up in the north-eastern part of the town, within a quarter of a mile of the Great Pond, Moswansicut, within a few rods of the boundaries of Scituate, Smithfield, Johnston and Glocester, almost on the line of junction of the four towns. The place lies about six rods from the road, and is indicated by a depression and raised banks. It was six or eight feet square, four or five feet deep, and raised above the ground by logs and branches of trees, some three or four feet. There was only one way of entrance, and holes were left in the upper part, through which a gun might be pushed to shoot bears, wolves, foxes, wildcats or other animals that might approach with design to enter the premises.

Tradition, handed down in the Mathewson families still resident in the neighborhood, further says: that Boston was at that time the nearest trading town, and thither, on foot, through Indian or other paths, John would make his occasional journeys, stopping at houses on the way. He made acquaintance with a Miss Malary at one of these houses where he stopped on his route, and offering marriage, was accepted. He built him a house a hundred yards or more from his cave, and cultivated a good farm. He died there, suddenly, aged about forty, leaving a widow and children. John, one of his sons, was the direct ancestor of the late Hon. Elisha Mathewson, senator in Congress.

Daniel, another son, when a boy of ten years, about the year 1700, was sent with a cart load of oak wood to Providence to sell. Two yokes of oxen and a horse were put in to draw the load over the rough and hilly road, and after driving all over the town to find a customer, he sold the load for five shillings, the most he could get. There were three houses only at that time on the north side of Westminster street, between the pumps and the forks of the road, by the bridge.

Thomas Mathewson and others of this name came to settle round this pond, one of the most beautiful ponds in the State, and having good lands around it. Elder Samuel Winsor owned a tract a little farther east of the pond, and his lands were said to reach to Providence. John Waterman, Dean Kimball and others were neighbors.

Mr. Stephen Smith kept tavern at the Four Corners, North Scituate, and as there was a great deal of teaming past his house, going to and returning from the furnaces of Smithfield and Glocester, to get iron ore at Cranston, his half-way house was well patronized.

Daniel Mathewson, the boy already spoken of, lived to about 1776, when he died at an advanced age. Noah, the son of Daniel, died Sept. 17, 1824, aged 89 years, and was buried by the side of his parents on the family lot. His widow, Judith, deceased Jan. 28, 1827, aged 87 years. The house that Daniel built was occupied successively, after his death, by his son Noah and his grandson Daniel, who was living in 1856 in his 78th year, and gave me this information of his family. Its height was one story, with four rooms on the ground floor, and a cellar underneath. In the old stone fire-place were seen hanging from a piece of timber, placed horizontally, high up in the chimney, two very long iron hooks or trammels, five or six feet long, for hanging kettles and other vessels over the fire. These were hoisted or lowered by means of little holes in the upper piece. They had no barns in those old times when this house was built, but there were little shanties or hovels where they stored many things.

James Aldrich removed to Scituate from Smithfield in 1775, and purchased of the heirs the estate of Mr. Ishmael Wilkinson, deceased. This was in the north-west part of the town, and in the vicinity of Beacon Hill. When Mr. Aldrich came to Scituate himself and family traveled on horseback, that being the usual mode of conveyance. Attempts were made to discourage him from leaving Smithfield by representing the lateness of spring, it being the middle of May, but as the land was good he declined to stop. Soon after his arrival he sent back to Smithfield to get a cheese tub made by a celebrated worker in wooden ware, Jesse Inches, who was known far and wide for his skill in manufacturing churns, pails and tubs. This cheese tub, made of cedar, held twenty pailfuls, which gives us some idea of the dairy of Mr. Aldrich, and of the cows about his premises. A stout man brought it on foot, and upon his back, all the way from Smithfield. It was sold at auction some seventy-five years after, on the breaking up of house-keeping by his son John, having been in the family three-quarters of a century.

The Smithfield people considered a journey to the adjoining town of Scituate, one hundred years ago, somewhat as we regarded a trip to Ohio some fifty years since; but quite a number of families and some very fine additions to the property, respectability and enterprise of Scituate, nevertheless, removed, and it may have been with a desire to keep them at home that the discomforts of Scituate were magnified. James Aldrich took the farm made vacant, as we have seen, by the unfortunate death of Mr. Wilkinson, and found the land pretty well prepared for culture—a comfortable house and barn, a good orchard, stone walls, good soil, and a very pleasant and healthful location.

Having a great taste for orcharding, which his son John imbibed, and his grandson Arthur inherited, who had the finest fruit in the town, he planted fruit trees for which the soil, climate and elevation of land were highly favorable, and became a successful farmer. He raised horses for sale, as was the custom then, and Scituate horses, for their fine qualities, were regarded at that time much as we regard those which are now brought from Vermont. He is said to have introduced the first cherry trees in the town.

Mr. James Aldrich was a great politician in those days, and belonged to the Republican or Democratic party, both names being

used at that time to designate the Jefferson party, in opposition to
the federal party of Hamilton. He represented the town of Scituate in General Assembly for one series of nineteen consecutive
years. Elisha Mathewson, John Harris and Col. Ephraim Bower
were often at his house, and Governor Arthur Fenner. The Governor used to come out of Providence on horseback, with his gun and
other equipments, to have a good hunt with his warm friend and
brother democrat, James. Dr. Battey told me he had seen them
hunting together when he was a boy, and a daughter of Mr. Aldrich,
Mrs. Charles Harris, remembered that many a time she had seen the
Governor ride away home from Scituate with foxes and squirrels
that he had killed, strung over his saddle.

Arthur must have loved the fun, and there was no very awful
state about a chief magistrate in those days to prevent his indul-
gence in a favorite sport. Political, as well as social and hunting
propensities, doubtless mingled in these expeditions, for Mr. James
Aldrich and his friend Elisha Mathewson were said to control the
votes of Scituate, and the people loved to see a Governor
among them in such a free and easy spirit and costume, and gladly
gave him the favor of their votes.

Women generally rode on horseback in these days, and favorite daughters were privileged with some fine horses to ride. Two
women were sometimes seen riding on one horse, each with a child
in her arms, but more frequently the "good man" with his wife behind him, going to church or to shopping in the small but thriving
village of Providence, which, in the first settlement, was indeed the
village of Scituate, as well as Providence.

Gideon Harris is a very prominent man in the history of Scituate. He married Damaus Wescott, a noted maiden in her day.
He died in 1777, at an advanced age, and was buried in the Quaker
burying ground. For many years he filled the office of Town
Clerk. It was a common saying that everybody who was poor, in
distress, or wanted employment, resorted to Mr. Harris, on account
of his property, influence and benevolent disposition. His house
was in a place called the "Old Bank." It was enlarged and made

into two stories by his son, and pleasantly situated on ground rising from the road, with its stately and ancient button-wood and elm trees, makes an imposing appearance.

JOSEPH WILKINSON AND THE HOPKINS FAMILY.

About the year 1703, Mr. Joseph Wilkinson, a son of Capt. Samuel Wilkinson, Esq., of Providence, came to live in the northwest part of Scituate, known by its Indian name, Chapumishcook. He married Martha Pray, a grand-daughter of one of the first settlers in the town. There was a crooked road leading from Providence to this neighborhood at this time. The first barn built in what is now Scituate was erected by him. He also brought the first cow into the town, and a piece of meadow where he pastured his cow, a little north, running into Foster, where the first hay was cut, had been created, it is supposed, by a beaver dam in the vicinity, causing an overflow of water and rotting the trees so that they fell down and gave an opportunity for the grass to grow.

Mr. Wilkinson was a surveyor, and much employed in this work in the town. In a deed of 1738 the surveyor's return was made under his hand. His residence was on the estate improved afterward by his great grandson, John Harris, Esq., in the most northern turnpike, a pleasant spot and a valuable farm. At the raising of his barn men came from Smithfield and Glocester to assist the Scituate people in its raising. When they had raised it they all sat down upon a large log and drank metheglin, a beverage made of honey and water and fermented, often enriched with spices. Some eighty years ago an old man named Hopkins, nearly eighty years of age, who was at this raising, and had a fresh recollection of the event, came along, and related it to the family resident there, and stated his participation in it. The barn had been taken down a little while before he came.

The house now standing on this farm is quite a large one, as are also the barns. The house has been twice repaired and enlarged by additions, but no part of the old Wilkinson house is retained in it. Two magnificent chestnut trees are standing in a lot opposite the house, of apparent great age.

Some anecdotes connected with his wife, whose maiden name was Martha Pray, illustrate the perils and heroism of the early settlers. Her husband, being absent at work some two miles off, she discovered a bear upon a sweet apple tree, shaking off the fruit that he might devour it on the ground. As it was the only tree of the kind they had, and highly valued, Mrs. Wilkinson not a little regretted the absence of her husband, whose gun kept loaded for such emergencies, was in its place on the pegs at the side of the wall. The apples continued to fall and rattle on the ground, and there was no other help at hand but the gun, which Martha, in a fit of desperation, took into her hands and going out the door which stood open, she took aim and fired. Dropping the gun on the ground immediately after the discharge, alarmed and trembling at what she had done, she ran back into the house and shut the door, afraid to look back and see what she had done, or the effect of the shot. When Mr. Wilkinson returned home, and was informed by his wife of what she had done, he went out to the tree and found the bear dead on the ground, so that his faithful and resolute wife had not only saved the cherished apples, but had secured some good meat as a supply.

This young married couple had also to guard their sheep by night from bears and wolves by putting them in log enclosures near the house. On one occasion they were awakened by a bear rolling the logs away in order to get at the sheep, and had to get up and drive him away.

Another incident called for his wife's coolness, courage and wisdom. Roving Indians sometimes called at the houses of the first settlers—a large party called at Mr. Wilkinson's house when none but his wife was at home. From their appearance, as she could not understand their language, she guessed that they wanted food, and she gave them all the provision she had in meat and meal. They took it and withdrew into a field near, made a fire and cooked and ate what had been given them, with great relish. It was no small relief to Mrs. Wilkinson, though she manifested no alarm, when they took their departure.

They came back after a few days and brought some fine venison, which they left, apparently as a return for Mrs. Wilkinson's favors, and as an expression of their grateful sense of her kindness. In this way a friendship was created with the Indians, and they were often welcome and happy inmates of the Wilkinson household, and brought their baskets, moccasins and manufactures to barter off for food and other things which they wanted.

Mr. Wilkinson appears prominent in the first town meeting of Scituate after it was set off from Providence. He is called Lieut. Wilkinson, was elected a member of the Town Council and chosen Deputy.

Mr. William Hopkins, the only child of Major William Hopkins, of Providence, married Ruth Wilkinson, daughter of "Capt. Samuel Wilkinson, Esq.," as he was styled in public records, and immediately after his marriage removed to a farm in Scituate in the neighborhood of Lieut. Joseph Wilkinson, the brother of his wife. His house was small, but the land was good—probably, not much cleared for tillage—in 1765, or thereabouts, when he took the place.

He is not much spoken of in the town records, and probably did not seek office, but gave himself steadily to the work of his farm and the care of his family. His memory is chiefly connected with some of his children who became illustrious and reflected great honor on their parents, and on the state and nation. William was the first born. He went abroad, and was presented at the court in England, and so took the favor of the King from his fine manly appearance, that he was appointed Major by him. A part of the coat he wore at court has been preserved by his descendants, and I have seen it on exhibition at one of the late antiquarian exhibitions in Providence. His other children were Stephen, John, Eseck, Samuel, Hope, Abigail and Susanna.

Eseck, soon after the death of his father, in the summer of 1738, a stout, tall and handsome young man, then in the twentieth year of his age, bid adieu to the old homestead and journeyed to Providence and became a sailor, soon rising to the position of Captain. He married when he was twenty-five years of age, Miss Desire Burroughs, daughter of Mr. Ezekiel Burroughs, of Newport, and took up his residence there. His conspicious services in the war of the revolution, as the first commodore of the navy are well known. His fleet, consisting of the ships Alfred, Capt. Dudley Saltonstall, and the Columbus, Capt. Whipple, the brig Andrew Doria, Capt. Nicholas Biddle, and the Cabot, Capt. John B. Hopkins, son of Eseck, and the sloops Providence, Fly, Hornet and Wasp, put out to sea Feb. 17, 1776, with a smart north-east wind, and cruising among the Bahama Islands, captured the forts at New Providence, Nassau. This was a very fortunate affair, for the heavy ordinance and stores taken proved quite acceptable to the country. He captured two British armed vessels on his return.

The Commodore, or Admiral, as Washington addressed him, met with difficulties in creating an efficient navy, and his force was wholly inadequate to protect the long line of coast and meet the vessels of the English navy, and he soon resigned and engaged in private armed vessels, as did his lieutenant, the famous John Paul Jones. He was successful in capturing many British vessels. In the collections of the Rhode Island Historical Society is a French engraving of him, which has a splendid figure and a handsome open countenance. It was circulated in France and this country in the early part of the war. The Commodore's family clock has been presented to Brown University, by his grand-daughter, Miss Elizabeth Angell. He died in 1802, and was buried at North Providence.

Stephen Hopkins was still more distinguished than the Commodore. He was born March 7, 1707. But little is known of his boyhood, but he must, with the other sons of William, been early taught to labor on the farm. There were no schools in his day, but his mother was a woman of marked talents and character, and no doubt instructed him in many things. It has come down to us that he inherited his abilities from her. His uncle Wilkinson, the surveyor, probably instructed him in that art, for we find him, still a youth, engaged in surveying. A strong passion for reading characterized his mature life. I was permitted to examine his library, which was large and valuable for the time. It would be interesting to know what books he read when a boy—procured at home, or obtained from connections and friends,—scarce, they probably were, and mostly of a religious character, but we may be sure he searched them thoroughly. Other means of culture were at hand. The conversation of parents, of visitors at his father's house, with visits to other families, added to his store of knowledge. Letters were arriving from England ; men and boys were returning from voyages at sea. Rhode Island being quite a maritime place, a minister would occasionally arrive from abroad and preach at a private house. If the school master passed through the place he may have said something. What other means had the boy Stephen Hopkins of education? Nature spread before him a beautiful panorama. His father's house, built on high land, overlooking a wide extent of country, presenting a succession of wooded summits, rounded in the blue sky, the aspect of the heavens, radiant at night,. and the seasons,

> " Whither the blossom blows, the summer ray
> Russets the plain, inspiring autumn gleams,
> Or winter rises in the blackening east."

all teaching some important lesson, and moulding the character : thus grew up that youth, who became fond of poetry, and the author of some fine pieces, which have been preserved. I have stood upon the spot where the birth place of this signer of the Declaration of Independence drew out my thoughts to consider the localities of the place as sending their influences to act upon his childhood. The foot-worn paths to the well, to the barn, and to the road, on account of a change of houses, the old one being much smaller, and built a little on the one side of the present structure, are not discernible. The garden in front of the house, on the opposite side of the road, and the family burying place, just outside of the garden walls, reach back to ancient times. The graves of successive residents are there, but no lines are on the stones that mark the last resting place of William and Ruth Hopkins, the parents of Governor and Admiral Hopkins. Would it not be well for the town of Scituate, on this centennial year, to put up in that ground a monument of honor and gratitude to the memory of those parents?

Stephen Hopkins married, June 27, 1726, Sarah, the youngest daughter of Major Silvanus Scott, of Providence. He married early, being only nineteen years of age—his wife was about the same age. To create a home and a support for the newly married ones, the father of Stephen made him a gift of seventy acres of land, and his grandfather, Thomas Hopkins, bestowed upon his "loving grandson," as the will reads, an additional grant of ninety acres. The grandfather of Sarah was Mr. Richard Scott, of Providence, "gentleman," the term used to show his quality.

Four years after this marriage, the portion, now Scituate, was set off from Providence, and Stephen Hopkins, then only twenty-three years of age, was the Moderator chosen. This fact is significant of the very high opinion entertained of him in his native town, as a man of business and competent to preside over public meetings. Joseph Brown was chosen Town Clerk for the first year, an office which included the registration of deeds, and Stephen Hopkins was elected the year after, and this office he held for ten successive years, and then resigned.

Mr. Hopkins removed to Providence in 1744, and purchased an estate on South Main street, at the corner of what is now Hopkins street, named after him, but formerly Bank lane, because the first bank in Rhode Island was located at the foot of it.

He engaged in commerce at Providence, but was soon called to fill important places in the State, as Chief Justice and Governor, —appointed to the Judgeship in 1739. No man was so often chosen as Moderator of Town Meetings in Providence. He assisted astronomers in making observations on the transit of Venus, at Providence, having a high mathematical reputation. His zeal for liberty led him in early life, and later, to write and publish papers on the "Rights of the Colonies," and to hold correspondence with distinguished patriots in various parts of the land. His memory was very retentive, and his capacity great. He died July 13, 1785.

Stephen Hopkins may stand forth as a representative of Rhode Island. Born and educated there amid hardships and perils, and believed in and honored by its people; his whole life, as it were, spent within its boundaries, and in its service, in the critical and forming period of its history, he represents its people.

Connected with the early settlers of this colony, on both the paternal and maternal sides; his birth reaching back to its simplest or rudest condition, and forward to the close of the American Revolution; his long, active, conspicuous life, spent among its people, moving and acting among them in constant and intimate contact with all classes and denominations, in domestic relations, business operations, and political and religious actions; assisting in framing, interpreting and executing their laws, and trusted by them with almost every office in their gift, we may consider him as a fair specimen of native growth, showing all the capabilities of soil and culture.

·It is to the honor of Rhode Island that she produced Stephen Hopkins; that he was the son of immigrants who selected her territory for a home, and that he was cradled, nurtured, approbated, exalted, and kept in public service so long, with her full consent and honest pride. The existence of such a man under such circumstances may certify, as a volume of true history may declare, to the character of her settlers and the influence of her institutions. There were true men and women who sought an asylum and built their homes on the Narragansett Bay; and they were not wanting in mental power, moral principle and heroic devotion to duty.

If these settlers maturing in their own native soil, and from their own native seed, had produced no other evidence of their worthiness to take an honorable place with the other New England colonies, the production of Stephen Hopkins would of itself suffice. He was a working man, beginning early and continuing late, covering half a century with his record of diligence.

His farming and mercantile operations absorbed much of his time and thought and strength. The business of surveying in the rough country in which he lived involved much hardship and labor, and he had much of it to perform. He was early engaged in attempts to develop the resources of the State in mining. His public life made him the servant of all ; and he was a close and severe student, filling up all the spare hours of his life with reading. The town records of Scituate attest that he was familiar with drudgery, and his committee labors in Congress won for him the praise of John Adams, as a business man. He owed much to his fine natural gifts, to the reputation and assistance of his family connections, and to the open field which Rhode Island offered at the time to a man of talent, tact and ambition—all three of which he possessed. But he, nevertheless, was indebted to his close application, indefatigable labor, and resolute persistence in toil, for his advancement. He thought it not beneath him to perform well the humblest duty, to execute faithfully the smallest trust, to excel in little things, and he never dreamed of idleness as his portion, or conceived that he could float into public favor and maintain influence without exertion. He had a small and obscure position, like a rill on a wooded mountain side, but he worked himself out of it, despite of obstacles, and became like a river growing wider and wider as it proceeded from its source to the place where it passed into the sea.

He was one of the people at all periods of his history. He had long been placed over them in office, but he never outgrew his place among them, and never lost his sense of fellowship and sympathy with the toil, exposure and privations of the humblest citizen. His heart beat responsive to the hearts of men ; he was ever fighting their battles, considering them as his own ; therefore it was that he had such a weight of influence—such a power of directing movements, and dared to act with so much decision. As an Illustration of his readiness to bear his part in all the burdens of the people, we find his name, in 1757, heading a list of thirty-six men—his son George one of them—who were ready to march against the French and Indians, who had invaded the northern frontier, possessed themselves of Fort McHenry, and were carrying death and devastation on their way. The tidings of their retreat prevented the party from setting out.

In the taking of the Gaspee, in which his son, John B. Hopkins, took a leading part, Mr. Hopkins being Chief Justice he asked the advice of the Assembly what course he should pursue if the British government should demand the men who destroyed her. He was told to use his own discretion, to which he answered,— "Then, for the transportation for trial, I will neither apprehend any person by my own order, nor suffer any executive officer in the colony to do it."

In the North Burial Ground, of Providence, is his grave; and there his State has erected a monument to his memory, on which, with other commendations, is inscribed these words: "His name is engraved on the immortal record of the Revolution, and can never die."

The children of Stephen Hopkins were Rufus, the first child, born Feb. 10, 1727 ; John, the second son, was born Nov. 11, 1728. Ruth, the eldest daughter, was born in 1729, and named after her grandmother Hopkins. She died in infancy in 1731, and was buried in Scituate. Lydia, the fourth child, was born in 1732, and probably died young. Silvanus, the third son, was born Oct. 16, 1734. Simon was born Aug. 25, 1736, and George, the seventh and youngest. child, was born in 1739. All the sons except Simon, who died while a lad, were sailors, going to sea while boys, and all became masters of vessels but Silvanus, who became mate at eighteen, and would have been captain soon after, had he lived. Rufus was so far successful that he invested five hundred pounds in the Hope furnace, Scituate, 1766, and became its superintendent. This furnace cast cannon which were used in the army and navy during the revolutionary war. There were two cannon usually cast at one time, and they were afterwards bored.

While living at the furnace he received the appointment of Judge, which he held for several years. He was one of a committee appointed by Congress, Dec. 14, 1775, to superintend the building of vessels of war. He was concerned in the first cotton factory put up near the Hope furnace in 1807. Silvanus, one of his sons, was the first agent of the Hope Manufacturing Company. Rufus

Hopkins died in August, 1809, at the house of Mr. Andrew Ralph, and was buried in the North Burial Ground, Providence. He is said to have greatly resembled his father, and the likeness in the picture of the signers of the Declaration of Independence, purporting to be that of Gov. Hopkins, is his.

Capt. John Hopkins, the second son of Stephen, in 1753, sailed for Cadiz, Spain, and died there July 20th, with the small pox, aged twenty-four years. Silvanus, the third son of Stephen was killed by Indians after he was cast away on the Cape Breton shore. Of the remaining children, Simon died at Providence, at the age of seven years, and George, the youngest, who married Ruth Smith, was lost at sea in the year 1775, with the vessel he commanded.

JOHN HULET, GOV. WEST, AND HUNTING GRAND OLD FURNITURE.

As the land was being cleared, with here and there, at irregular places, a clearing made or commenced,

"Where not a habitation stood before,
Abodes of men irregularly massed."

One of these, whose chimney smokes were illuminated by the morning sun in the woods of Scitaate, in its early settlement, was John Hulet and Berenice, his wife, who, about 1740, resided in the north-western part of the town. His grave is pointed out in a pasture back of the house of John Harris, Esq., a short hillock, marked by two walnut trees, and lying on the westerly side of the most northern one. Two rough moss-covered stones, one at each end of the grave, and without inscription, designate the last resting place of one who owned large tracts of land in the vicinity, but now sleeps unnoticed and unknown by the living generations about him. His transactions in deeds were numerous, and run from 1743 to 1763. In 1744 he bought one hundred and fifty acres of Stephen Hopkins for three hundred pounds, land commonly called "Oyster-shell Plain." We find him, among others, taking the oath against bribery, Aug. 15, 1747, an example which might be followed at the present day for the advantage of the country.

Benjamin Gorton, of Warwick, married John Hulet's daughter

Avis, July 18, 1762. His son Mason married, the year following, Oct. 23, 1763, Elizabeth Mathewson, of Johnston. Elder Reuben Hopkins performed the marriage service on both these interesting occasions. Mason Hulet removed to Vermont and settled at Wallingford, on the Otter Creek, and has left numerous descendants in that State. John Hulet, March 1761, sold to Col. Wm. West the farm of two hundred acres which he bought of Stephen Hopkins. He sold it for forty thousand pounds, a price not to be accounted for, except, we admit, the great depreciation of the currency. Mr. Hulet was appointed, with Thomas Angell, pound keeper, in 1747. He is called "Captain" in his appointment of fence viewer in 1750. He was undoubtedly a man of considerable property for those days, and quite a dealer in lands. He sold to Boylston Brayton, of Smithfield, May 28, 1763, two tracts of land,—one lying in Glocester, according to the deed, "the half of a farm whereon Ralph Wellman did formerly live, and bounded as in deed of William West to Eliphalet Eddy, Feb. 16, 1760, and also more particularly by the said Eddy to me, the said John Hulet, containing three hundred acres, more or less. The other tract is in Scituate, and is my homestead farm, and the same whereon I now dwell, and contains about two hundred and fifty acres, bounded northerly on land of James Wheeler, easterly on land of the same, and on land belonging to Capt. John Whipple, southerly on land of William West and westwardly on land of Charles Hopkins and Barnes Hall, and on land belonging to heirs of Joseph Wilkinson." This homestead farm would seem to have been very near to the place of his burial. We find him buying at the same time of Benj. Anthony, of Swanzea, for 1800 Spanish milled dollars, 229 1-2 acres of land, where Thomas·Knowlton once dwelt in Scituate, in part bounded by territory of heirs of Joseph Wilkinson. Mr. Hulet must have died soon after these last transactions, as we find no further mention of him in the town records. He is said to have died of fever after a very short illness.

Lieut.-Gov. West, who purchased the old homestead which Gov. Hopkins sold to John Hulet, had for some time previous to

1761, been living in Scituate, and had resided a little west of said farm, where his son John afterwards lived.   He removed from North Kingston to Scituate, and was chosen Deputy.   He was also elected to represent the town in a General Convention held at East Greenwich, Sept. 26, 1786.   In the appointment by the Governor in 1775, of Eseck Hopkins to be General of troops to be raised for the defence of the shores of the Narragansett, Col. West was placed second in command.   We find him very active in town affairs during the Revolutionary war.   In May, 1777, he was made chairman of a committee to ascertain the number of effective soldiers still wanting to complete the Continental battalion, then raising by the State.   He was several times chosen as Moderator of the town, and was a man of intelligence and enterprise, infusing energy and courage in the people.

In 1775 he put up the largest and most showy house that had ever been erected in Scituate.   Mr. Welcome Arnold, who died some twenty years ago, was at the raising of this house, and used often to speak of the great gathering and interest of the occasion. Liquors of all sorts were furnished, but while rum was very plentiful there was a choice kind of wine, of which the people were only permitted to take a *little.*   This house is on the Providence and Hartford turnpike, three miles west of the village of North Scituate.   It is a gambrel-roofed house of two stories as it fronts the' road, and of four stories on the end opening to the east, including the basement and the attic story.   The rooms in the house are very spacious, and the attic seems as large as many meeting houses, it being all in one room.   It was quite a museum, with old fashioned looms, spinning wheels, chests of drawers, and other articles, when I saw it.

A very interesting historical place is this house, built by Lieut. Gov. William West, coeval with our centennial year, and it is a very pleasant coincidence that one of our committee lives in the house with his brother-in-law, Mr. Richard A. Atwood.   I rather think that not a few rebels were quartered there at times in the Revolution, and seditious conversation indulged in, and even rebel-

lion openly talked of, and schemes devised against the British
troops and vessels.   I don't see why that house, built on the premises where Gov. Stephen Hopkins and Commodore Eseck Hopkins
were born, should not be placarded, these centennial days, with the
noble and patriotic words of Rhode Island statesmen and heroes
as is the case to-day with the Old South Church in Boston, and
flags and streamers displayed upon it.   The old house was raised
and built by patriotic men who knew how to handle the musket and
the sword, and doubtless did, most of them, serve in the American
army and navy.   If the old folks have gone to their reward in
heaven they have left us a memorial of their day, in this edifice,
and may it stand a century longer.

Gov. West was quite a farmer and kept a great many cows.
He would often set off with a load of cheese to sell, valued at $1,500.
He married Ellen Brown ; his children were William, Charles, John,
Samuel, Hiram, Elsie, Olive, Ellen, Sally and Hannah.   Job Ran-
dall married two of his daughters—Ellen for his first wife, and
Sally for his second.   Jeremy Philips married Elsie West, and
Hannah married Mr. Gideon Smith, father of Mr. Russel Smith,
who resides in North Scituate village.

The going down in value of continental money ruined Gov.
West financially, as it did many other patriots of the Revolution
who trusted the government, and made his last years afflictive.
This was one of the sacrifices our fathers made for us, that we might
enjoy freedom and prosperity.   Mr. West died about sixty years
ago.   Elder Westcott attended his funeral.   He was a man rather
above the middle height, a bony, sinewy man, long favored; with a
prominent nose.

As an illustration of the spirit of the town of Scituate, in the
Revolutionary war,   and   as   evidence   of   confidence   in   their
townsmen, are many votes on record.   Here is one!—" At a Town
Meeting held April 28, 1777, it was Voted that Col. William West
be appointed to use the utmost of his endeavors and abilities, by giving directions to his under-officers, as well as using his influence other
ways, to raise soldiers by enlisting the number of men assigned to

be raised in this town, by act of Assembly aforesaid." May 5,
following, he was chosen chairman of a committee "to prepare and
divide into classes the male inhabitants of the town, liable to bear
arms." How ready the town was to bear its proportion of war ex-
penses, see the following vote of September 23, 1779: "Voted
that the town will raise their proportion of the $20,000,000 recom-
mended by the Hon. Continental Congress, £5,359, 2s, 8d being
said town's proportion. The collector of taxes is directed to pay
the same, when collected, into the Loan Office in this State, taking
Loan Office certificates of the same."

In this part of the town, where Col. West lived, are preserved
some articles of furniture of great antiquity, heir-looms of families.
Mrs. Farnham, who lives on the road to the West House—a little
east—the only surviving child of the late Hon. Elisha Mathewson,
has in her possession the veritable looking-glass brought to Scituate by her first ancestor, John Mathewson. It is small—the plate
only seven inches by nine—of hard wood frame, stout, and of good
repair, save that the quicksilver has come off in a good many
small spots. The same lady has other centennial articles,—one is
a solid mahogany table of an oval form, three feet in length, an old
fashioned tea table. This table was brought from England, and it
belonged to Mrs. Farnham's grandmother, the wife of Richard
Smith, whose maiden name was Lydia Clarke, daughter of Judge
Joseph Clarke, who was driven off in the Revolutionary war to
Pawtuxet. Several ancient chairs are also the property of this
venerable lady, who is still living. The backs are about four and a
. half feet high, with leather bottoms and backs, with brass nails and
carved work on the top. These were brought from Newport, and
came from the same family as the table, and were made in England.
An old cane of her grandfather, Thomas Mathewson, with round
top and brass ferrule and bottom, is also preserved by this lady.
John Harris, Esq., had an oaken arm chair, rush-bottomed, made
by his grandfather, John Aldrich, during a great snow storm and
the time subsequent, in all three weeks, that the people were kept
from traveling. This chair commemorates a fall of snow unpara-

lelled in Rhode Island history, and probably dates back to the remarkable snow storms of 1716 or 1738. A silver cup, holding
about a pint, and reaching back to Jonathan Harris, great-grandfather of John, is in preservation to be handed in due course to
Stephen Harris, son of John, now in California. This cup was
originally left as a legacy to be thus transmitted from generation to
generation.

Mr. George Brownell left several articles of antiquarian value.
A table of curled maple, three feet across at the top, with slanting
legs crossing each other, once the property of his grandfather,
Samuel Aldrich, who came from England and settled in Smithfield.
It came subsequently into the hands of his son John, and his grandson James who settled in Scituate. There is a pewter soup platter
of the same hereditary origin, twenty inches across, very heavy,
marked with the initials of three generations—J. for John Aldrich,
S. for Samuel, E. for Elizabeth, wife of John, J. for Jane.

Simeon Arnold came from Smithfield, and purchased about
two hundred acres of land, including the farm on which his grandson, Simeon C. Arnold, now lives; he died about ninety-six years
ago, occupying the premises until his death. His son Dexter
was born, lived and died on the same farm, living as did his father
to the age of about eighty years. His son Simeon, now upwards of
fifty years old, has known no other home. He and his wife are
the sixth generation from Roger Williams.

Other families have more or less of tables; chests of drawers,
and chairs of ancient patterns, many of them still in use. The
quantity of pewter is considerable, and parts of antiquated China
sets are found here and there. Looking-glasses, a few large and
handsome ones, of great age, are to be found.

The spinning wheels, large and small, of former generations,
are placed away in garrets, or stored in old and dilapidated out-
buildings. Their busy hum is heard no longer, but silent, as those
who once used them in commendable skill and industry, we may
imagine them as wearing away life in indolent musings of the past,
and perhaps wonder if the wheels of fashion will ever bring them

again into favor. How many pleasant hours are associated in the past with these now neglected wheels. The spinning by them of wool, cotton and flax was esteemed an honorable and indispensable avocation. The young daughters of a household soon learnt with pride to survey the skeins of yarn they had spun, and many a charming day-dream was born in the monotonous buzz of the spinning wheel, and many a sweet song was sung by youth and beauty:

> "Noise sweetens toil, however rude the sound,
> All at her work the village maiden sings,
> Nor while she turns the giddy wheel around,
> Revolves the sad vicissitude of things."

. Every newly married couple must have a spinning wheel to commence life with, and the solitude of the new settlements was broken by the cheerful sound of the buzzing wheel. The old ladies solaced many a weary hour of the live-long summer day at this employment, the door thrown open, and the cooling breeze sporting with the rolls they were spinning into useful threads.

Considerable interest is attached to the table, platter and bureau, handed down from Samuel Aldrich, which have been mentioned, from the following anecdote, showing how they were saved from destruction: Mr. Aldrich, one of the first settlers of. Smithfield, had an Indian servant in his family. Several strange Indians came. along one day and had a talk with this servant in the Indian language, the purport of which he made known to his master after the strange Indians had gone away. He told Mr. Aldrich that King Philip had proclaimed war, and he advised him to remove immediately. Accordingly, they went to work, digging holes to bury their heaviest and most bulky articles ; and the most light and portable they took with them, the whole family proceeding in all haste to Providence. They were not any too swift, for on arriving at Tracy's Hill, in Johnston, they saw their house in flames, kindled by the Indians. They passed some armed Indians in their flight, but Mr. Aldrich's Indian, pointing to his master, said : "That man is my master; you must not kill him." Mr. Samuel Aldrich was a Quaker preacher.

Not very long ago in Scituate, no house was painted, plastered

or papered, there were no carpets—the parlor floors were sanded,
and hardly any furniture was in the house, and what was to be
seen was simple and rude.   A few ordinary chairs, rush-bottomed,
or in the case of the better sort, stuffed with straw and covered
with stout leather.   Tables, stoutly made, but rude in construction,
and bedsteads equally common and inelegant.   Trenchers, or wooden
plates, were in use in most families until the war of the Revolution,
and to some extent afterwards.   Pewter plates and earthen mugs,
with a little China, appeared after tea drinking came in fashion,
with cups and saucers very small.   The Chinaware was considered
so choice and genteel that it was placed in a little cupboard over
the fire-place, and the glass door or window in it enabled all
visitors to see the half-dozen or more ornamented cups.   Old looms,
now disused, remain to show how independent the farmer was in
those ancient times, wearing his home-made clothes and demonstrat-
ing the capabilities of his wife, who often in church on Sundays
eyed with just pride her husband's nicely spun and woven clothes,
the product of her own hands, and often the cutting and making of
them also.

   Edwin and his brother John Howland, living on and owning
extensive portions of land in the northerly section of Scituate,
sold to Jeremiah Smith of Providence, in 1788, one hundred and
seventy-five acres for $2,100, who put up on it a one-story gambrel
roof house, and died in 1816, aged ninety-two years.   Mr. Martin
Smith, his great-grandson, occupied a large two-story house, built
by his father in 1817.

   Richard Brown, living in Providence, attracted by the fine
situation of the land for hunting grounds, procured, so tradition
says, at about the cost of laying out and registering, a large tract
of land.   Richard Brown, Jr., June 5th, 1765, gave to his son
Jesse two hundred acres, saying: "it is the lot of land given to
me by my grandfather, Richard Brown, April 28, 1744, and is on
Mosquito Hawk Plain."   Jesse settled on the spot, and also his
brother Samuel.   Mr. William Brownell, and after him Isaac S.
Devereaux, of Providence, bought and lived there.

Richard Brown, the senior, lived to be an hundred years old. As his century birthday approached, his children and friends made great preparations to celebrate the day by a dance and a feast. As the old gentleman was still hearty and active, they got him out to dance, and enjoying the sport as well as any one, he exerted himself to comply with the general wish, making much merriment and acquitting himself well. He did not live long afterwards.

A hunting house, or lodge, was built nearly a century and three-quarters ago, for the convenience of sportsmen from Providence and other places, while hunting deer and other game in that then wild and unsettled region. These animals used to come to the hunting house brook to drink, and in the thick tangled wood and brush, and tall herbage, they found a covert, and tender grass and berries for food. Some of the gentlemen who resorted to this place for hunting were Joseph Smith, Richard Brown, Jeremiah Smith, Edward Howland, John Hulet, Joseph Wilkinson, William West, James Aldrich and Gov. Fenner.

A famous squirrel hunt took place about 1784, on a wager between the towns of Glocester and Scituate, as to which should kill the greatest number. They were to hunt for ten successive days and then bring in the spoils and make the award. Judges were mutually appointed, consisting of a committee of fifteen. Ten gallons of rum and the expense of a dinner for the committee was to be the forfeit of the losing party.

The boys turned out as well as the men, and even the women became fired with ardor. The dogs entered heartily into the work of searching the woods and ferreting out the squirrels. The squirrels were taken by surprise, at such a general, earnest and murderous onslaught, the object of which they so little understood. Doubtless, many Revolutionary soldiers, fresh from the battle-fields, condescended to show their skill on this occasion. At the close of the period allotted for shooting, the company met at the house of James Aldrich, to decide who were the victors. The piles of the respective combatants were ranged on each side of the town's border line opposite to each other, and consisted of the heads and one of the fore-paws of each of the slaughtered animals. The heaps were about the size of hay cocks. Scituate beat Glocester by several thousands. Mr. Obediah Fenner, of Foster, was present, and related to me these facts.

THE ANGELL TAVERN AND OTHER PUBLIC HOUSES.

Thirty-five years ago there stood very near the geograpical centre of Scituate, in a place latterly known as Richmond Mills, an antique and somewhat grotesque edifice of a century and a quarter's date, looking very much the worse for time, with its red paint nearly all washed off, and looking dingy enough, and a little awkward with its south-east corner projecting very near to the junction of two roads. That was our old "Angell Tavern," built when the stumps in the road, and the wide-spreading forest around, indicated a country just beginning to be cleared up. When it was raised, so few were the inhabitants around, that they had to send to Providence for men to assist; there was a great gathering of the region for many miles in circuit, and a merry time they had of it, and also when the tavern sign was elevated and the house opened for public entertainment. A curious and entertaining history is belonging to that old house, for town meetings were held there, and the news of the day proclaimed, and politics discussed, and strangers found there a good supper and a night's lodging. It was two stories high, with the eaves of the front extending a few feet, forming a little shelter in stormy weather. On the western end was a very huge stone-chimney, forming a wall for that end of the building. There was also back of the main building, an addition sloping down from the main roof to form a kitchen, closet and bed-room, one story high, which being old and out of repair, was taken down in 1823. The house had three-narrow windows, with small panes of glass on the lower front, and four of the same description above, with one at the east end. The front door was at the western extremity of the part facing on the road. As you entered, a door on the right hand of the passage opened upon the bar-room, a large square room, and leading out of it, the entire length of the remaining fore part of the house was a sitting-room, used in later years, if not before, for a bed-room. Back of the bar-room was a kitchen, a large square room, which had been as large again before the addition was removed. A bed-room was at one end of it, nearly corresponding in size to the sitting-room, directly behind which it stood. The only pair of stairs to the upper rooms, ascended from the kitchen at the west end. Three bed-rooms were on the east end, and all the rest of the second floor, with the exception of a sleeping chamber over the front entry, was a hall for dancing and public meetings.

I have been thus minute and full in this description, as this tavern is often referred to in the doings at Scituate—a sort of town hall, exchange, eating and lodging house, real estate office, and place of resort for young and old, day and evening, where bargains were made, balls were held, and a general news-room established, or what was equivalent to it.

Capt. Thomas Angell, who built this house one hundred and sixty-six years ago, that is, in 1710, if a stone, taken out of the chimney, gives the correct date, was a large owner of property in the vicinity, and had built his first house of much smaller dimensions and in simpler construction, near where Pardon Angell's house stands, a quarter of a mile north. His land lay on both sides of the Ponagansett river, and his second house was erected near a fall of water, improved of late years for a factory, but might originally have been used for a saw and grist mill. Immediately before the tavern the river makes rather a sudden bend, rounding with a graceful sweep through woodlands festooned with vines, which still grow in the region. Before the house, on the opposite or southern side, the land sloped down to a very beautiful intervale on the sides of the stream.

The parties taking possession of this new house were the family of Capt. Thomas Angell. He was the son of John and Ruth Angell, of Providence, and was born March 25, 1672, and married April 4, 1700, Sarah Brown, daughter of Daniel Brown and Alice his wife. Sarah was born at Providence, Oct. 10, 1677. It must have been very soon after their marriage that the young and adventurous couple took up their line of march for the thousand acres of wild land, of which Thomas had become the proprietor.

In 1730 Scituate was taken out of the limits of Providence and made a separate town. The first meeting it was voted to hold the town meetings in the new house of Capt. Thomas Angell. Three years afterwards he was appointed to represent the town in the General Assembly. He contracted with the town to build a bridge over Ponagansett river in 1734, and about the same time he petitioned with one or two others to have a pound near his dwelling, and leave was granted that they might do it at their own expense, which they did, building it of stone. It stood two or three rods east of the tavern, and continued to be the only pound in the town until 1810, when the place being wanted by Mr. Charles Angell, the then proprietor of the tavern, to put up a new and spacious house upon the spot, it was removed and a new one built on the opposite side of the road, a little west of the old spot.

The town meetings continued to be held at Mr. Angell's tavern for many years, until the building of the Baptist Church a mile east. The large hall in the second story was improved on these occasions. By far the largest use of the hall was for dancing. This tavern became quite noted among the traveling community, and what is remarkable, continued in the hands of the family until quite recently, except a period of ten years, during the ill-health of Mr. Andrew Angell, when it was leased successively to John Manchester, Nathan Manchester and Mr. Hazard. Mr. Charles Angell then resumed it on the old hereditary line.

Many eminent men have been entertained at this tavern, as well as a multitude of more humble travelers. Gen. Washington has stopped there. Gen. Lafayette encamped his regiment on the pleasant intervale in front of the house while marching through the town during the Revolutionary war. They continued there until the troops had finished their washing in the river. The old people used to speak often to their children about the fine music of the band, as in the morning and evening they played in the camp. Lafayette lodged in the tavern, and another French officer of high rank had accommodations in a house near by, where lived Mr. Abel Angell. Mr. Angell's wife, who died thirty-five or forty years ago, used to speak of making porridge for this officer, whom she called General, while he was sick at her house. This house stood for a long period, and Mr. Richard Angell, son of Abel, pointed out to myself and other visitors the small bed-room back of the kitchen which had been occupied by the officer. Gen. Lafayette, on his last visit to this country, passed up the same road, recognized the old places, and enquired particularly for a spring at the foot of Cranberry Hill, some three or four miles west of the Angell tavern on the turnpike, at which spring he and his troops had refreshed themselves on their dusty and weary march. Many were then alive to greet him, of his old companions in the war. Dr. Owen Battey, residing within a mile of the tavern, on the same road, remembered seeing Lafayette and his soldiers as they passed along, and also of walking into the camp-ground on the intervale, led, while a child, by one of his father's men.

It being in the fall of the year the river was high, and one of the soldiers having drunk too freely tried to drown himself, but other soldiers jumped into the river and pulled him out.

Some things remain of the old tavern. The well which faithfully served other generations abides to moisten the lips of several families in the neighborhood, and gives a good supply for all household uses. The old stone steps, as good as new, upon which so many feet alighted from travelers' carriages, and the ponderous iron shovel for the use of the oven, are still in use. A hatchet which once belonged to Jeremy Angell, and marked February, 1755; an iron square, bearing the date April 2, 1770, and formerly the property of Andrew Angell, and a gauge of still greater antiquity, for measuring the contents of barrels, are still preserved, or were up to twenty years ago, when I saw them; but the hatchet, once so indispensable in a household, for the preparation of flax for use, is no longer wanted. The large old clock that clicked in the bar-room has been swapped away for a smaller and more modern measurer of time. A chest of drawers belonging to old Capt.

Thomas Angell, who first occupied the tavern, was burnt up forty-five years ago in the house of Mr. Stephen Peckham, which was destroyed by fire. One or two tables of ancient form are left, but time and accident have swept away other articles of furniture.

In a field back of the house is a burial place containing the graves of some of the ancient household. Mr. Andrew Angell, who died about 1791 ; his wife, Tabitha, who survived thirty years and deceased Dec. 10, 1821; Gideon Angell, son of Andrew, who was born June 21, 1773, and died unmarried, May 14, 1829; Abigail Hopkins, brought up by Andrew Angell, and who married a Sanders. The last named grave, with that of him who brought her up, is without an inscription.

Capt. Angell seems to have made his tavern the great centre of business and amusement in the town. The militia musters were held in the vicinity, and the pound drew all the stray cattle, and their owners to reclaim them ; there, too, the blacksmith shop adjoining the pound, under another line of Angells, brought customers, and there also, we must not forget to mention, was the "stocks," a machine consisting of two heavy pieces of timber, rounded so as to enclose the legs of criminals, and in which ludicrous and painful condition they had to sit out their time. Here, too, those who got into scrapes during the trainings, and at other times, were put; and the pole of the tavern sign was used as a post to fasten those unfortunate gentlemen who were sentenced to be whipped, an operation they were not likely very soon to forget.

Other taverns sprung up, as the town increased, in different places. Matthew Manchester was licensed as an inn-keeper in 1769, and Thomas Manchester and Levi Colvin at the same time. Stephen Smith and Zebedee Hopkins were licensed in 1762, and Col. John Potter and Christopher Potter in 1760. Some of these persons lived in Foster, then a part of Scituate.

Peter Cook, 1755; Joseph Kimball, 1745; Jeremiah Angell, 1758; Elisha Hopkins, jr., 1758; William West, 1758; John Hulet, 1745; Thomas Brown, 1749; Samuel Cooper, 1745; Henry Randall, jr., 1748; William Jackson, 1758, were among the licensed.

"Tavern Ale House and Victualling House" is the term employed in licensing many of the above. Only a few of these persons could have done much business.

An old house on Bald Hill, marked on the chimney 1710, or 1740, was built by John Hammond, who lived in it; also Jeremiah Baker lived there, and died about forty years ago.

The license to Joseph Knight runs thus: "License to keep a tavern, or house of public entertainment, and to retail strong liquors in said town, and hath given bond for maintaining good order and conforming to the regulations of the law respecting taverns and public houses. Provided, that he suffer no unlawful game or games, drunkenness, or any other disorder, in said house, or in any place in his possession, but that good government, rule and order be kept therein according to law." This license is dated Feb. 12, 1803, and is signed, John Harris, Clerk.

Thomas Wilmarth, who was a tavern keeper and clothier, kept an old tavern, still standing. His son, Stephen Wilmarth, of Glocester, married Nancy, daughter of James Aldrich.

The first tavern in Providence, and the first in the State, was in May, 1638, in charge of William Baulston.

Two taverns in each town, in early legislation, were allowed, and leave was granted to add one more if they saw fit: this was in 1655. Very full laws were enacted regulating the sale of liquors. The tavern bars were to be closed at 9 o'clock in the evening. Tavern keepers, when they trusted any one for liquors beyond twenty shillings, were barred an action at law.

We are very liable to undervalue country taverns in these days of their decline. In a newly settled country they are pioneers, and the house of the first settler becomes of a necessity the inn or lodging place of the traveler. As the settlement increases and the traveling multiplies, the tavern becomes a real estate office, where land is bought and sold. Inasmuch as there were no newspapers in circulation, and no post office, the tavern became the centre of information for those who were shut out by a residence in the woods, from tidings of the world. Macauley, in his History of England, says that tavern keeping was most flourishing as to patronage and being well kept when the roads were in the poorest condition, and traveling slow and laborious.

Daniel Webster's father, building his house on the farthest line of civilization, in New Hampshire, could not well help being a tavern keeper, and his son Daniel was favored with more avenues of information by reason of it than the boys not so privileged in new settlements.

The old Angell tavern is well represented to-day in Mr. James B. Angell, the popular president of Michigan University.

Capt. Thomas Angell's children were Jeremiah, Nehemiah, Isaiah, Jonathan, Thomas, Martha and Sarah—all Scripture names. Every one but Jonathan married and had children. Dividing his lands, he gave large farms of two hundred acres to each of his sons, and built handsome houses of two stories high for four of them, and a smaller house for Jonathan. Two of these houses remain. The daughters, no doubt, received gifts. At their father's death in 1744, Martha inherited by his will a negro girl called Phillis, and Sarah a negro boy named James.

Thomas, the youngest son, was the executor of his father's will. Jeremiah followed his father in the keeping of the tavern, and was a highly respectable man. He was a Justice of the Peace as early as 1741, and was afterwards Town Treasurer. His first wife was Mary Mathewson, his second Abigail Graves, and his third Elizabeth Stow. He died in 1786, aged seventy-nine years, having been born January 29, 1707. His widow survived till December 10, 1821.

Nehemiah Angell, second son of Thomas, married Mary Hopkins, sister to Elder Reuben Hopkins. He had three sons, Pardon, Nehemiah and Abraham, and his daughters were four, namely: Zilpah, Martha, Mercy and Mary. A grandson, Mr. Pardon Angell, became the owner of the farm, and soon after took down the old one-story red house, and put up a new one. Isaiah, the third son, married Miss Wilkinson, and had only one daughter, named Prudence, who married Gideon Austin, and had a large family. ·

Thomas Angell, jr., married Mercy, and had one daughter, Sally, who married a Sterry. Mr. Angell sold out and removed to Providence. Martha Angell married Mr. Knight, and Sarah married Jeremy Mathewson, on the very day the Angell tavern was raised. The children of Jeremiah were brought up with their father in the tavern. Daniel, born August 16, 1748, went to sea unmarried, and did not return. Andrew, one of his sons, married Tabitha Harris, daughter of Gideon Harris, Esq., and carried on the tavern after his father.

SCITUATE IN THE REVOLUTIONARY WAR.

From the character of the men who settled in Rhode Island it might be expected that they would be quick and energetic in resisting all encroachments upon their liberties, and such was the case. The taking of the Gaspee was the earliest resistance by arms to the power of Great Britain in any of the colonies. Great sympathy was awakened for the people of Boston, under the vexatious and vindictive treatment of England, and supplies were voted in all the Rhode Island towns, and sent for their relief.

When the news of the battle of Lexington arrived at Providence a thousand men were on the march the next day for the scene of conflict, but were countermanded by expresses from Lexington.

The Rhode Island forces, incorporated with the grand army before Boston, were placed under the direction of Washington. Rev. William Emerson, of Concord, chaplain in the army, who saw them at Cambridge in 1775, describing the military camps there, from various places, and noticing the want of tents and arms and apparel of many of the companies, says of some proper tents and marquees: "In these are the Rhode Islanders, who are furnished with tent equipage and everything in the most exact English style."

But it was not always so. Two years later, Aug. 27, 1777, Col. Israel Angell writing from the camp to the Governor of Rhode Island, declares that "pure necessity urges me to write you of the wretched condition of my command, as to their clothing and equipments. Only one half of the men are fit for duty, and many are barefoot." At another time, of some companies, it was said:

"There are not two in five who have a shoe or stocking, or other apparel to make them decent. But they rendered good service at Brandywine a month afterwards, contributing to a very important victory. Washington said of them: "The gallant behavior of Col. Angell's regiment on the 23d of June, at Springfield, reflects the highest honor upon the officers and men: they disputed an important pass with so obstinate a bravery that they lost upwards of forty in killed and wounded and missing—nearly one-fourth of their number, before they gave up their ground to a vast superiority of force.

Job and Joseph Angell, twin brothers, born January 19, 1745, were out in arms during the whole of the Revolutionary war. Job commanded a company but did not go out of the State. He has a son Job living in Scituate. Joseph Angell continued a private soldier, refusing offers of promotion, and distinguished himself in the war. He was with Washington the greater part of the war and fought in many battles. The old people that knew him had memories very quick to remember "Uncle Joe," the old soldier, who made a good impression on their minds. He used to relate tales of the war and events in the battles of which he was one of the actors. At the battle of Monmouth, the day being very hot, the men after the action flung themselves down by the river to drink, and many of them died in consequence, and indeed many were so faint that they died where they laid down, without drinking. Capt. Boss, Joseph's captain, laid down completely exhausted, until some one came and raised him up to drink spirits. Gen. Washington rode in among the troops ordering them not to drink without first tasting some spiritous liquor. Joseph said he always kept a little in his canteen for such a purpose, and he had so reserved some for himself in that battle. In the fight at the Red Bank on the Jersey shore, when the Hessians unsuccessfully attacked Fort Mercer, and were so cut up by the fire of the Americans, Joseph loaded and fired his gun for forty minutes as fast as he could, and without a moment's cessation until his gun became so hot that he could not hold it in his hand.

At a time during the war, when an engagement was about to commence, a cannon-ball from the enemy struck an apple tree in the road, taking off a branch. Washington, who was near, pleasantly remarked: "That was a good shot." Accounts agree that Joseph really loved the soldier's profession, that he engaged in it with his whole heart, and conducted himself bravely during the whole war. When peace was declared he returned to Scituate to take up once more the plough. He selected a daughter of John Edwards for his wife, and had two sons, Jonathan and Israel, who both married and removed to the State of New York.

Joseph Knight acted an important part in the Revolutionary war. His father, Jonathan Knight, executed to him the lease of his farm for six years, April 4th, 1763, Jeremiah and Andrew Angell witnessing the same. He appears to have used his teams extensively in transporation for Hope furnace.

From papers in the possession of his descendants, which have been kindly loaned me, we get much information of Revolutionary times. He seems to have had a taste early for military life, having received from Gov. Samuel Ward, June 16th, 1766, a commission as Ensign of the First Company, or Trained Band, of Providence. He was made Lieutenant of the same company, in 1769, and in August, 1774, he was created Captain. April, 1775, after the news of battle of Lexington, a company was formed in Scituate under him as captain, the roll headed thus: " We do enlist ourselves as Volunteers in the present emergency in defence of our country and Right of Privileges and Liberty." Four new companies were chartered in Scituate, Dec. 5, 1774, and one of them was called "Scituate Hunters."

A letter from Gov. Cooke to Joseph Knight, dated Providence, Dec. 19, 1775, directed to him as captain of the second company of minute men in Scituate, says: " You are hereby directed to gather together the company under your command with all possible expedition and march them to this town in order to be transported to Rhode Island for the defence of that island. You are to be careful that the men are properly equipped with arms, ammunition and blankets fit for immediate service. I have advice from Gen. Washington that eight large transports, with two tenders, having on board one regiment of foot, and three companies of horse sailed from Boston last Saturday, and I have no doubt that your officers and men will exert themselves upon this occasion with their usual ardor."

Gov. West sends an order from head-quarters to Capt. Knight, Jan. 12, 1776, for nine privates with a commissioned officer and sergeant or corporal, upon fatigue duty. Ten days afterwards Gen. Lippitt directs him, from Prudence, to send ten men up there to go in a scow down to the Pearl. The men sent were in the fight at Prudence.   According to the record they were, Joseph Knight, captain ; William Brownell and Simeon Wilbour, sergeants ; Abraham Angell, corporal ; and Joseph Turner, Stephen Leach, Oliver Leach, Oliver Fisk, Zebedee Snow, Christopher Edwards, Joseph Wight, Moses Colvin, and Christopher Knight.

Providence was threatened by the enemy and Scituate was called upon to assist in its defence. Gen. Sullivan writes to Mr. Knight, who has been promoted to be Lieut.-Colonel, to march immediately with his regiment to their aid : " Pray, delay no time, for by the delay of one hour we may lose the town of Providence ; let each man take three days provision, and wait there for further orders."   About this time, March 18, 1777, Elizabeth Knight writes from Scituate to her husband, who was with his troops at Warwick : "These lines are to let you know that we are all well at present. I want you to come home soon as you can, to see about getting some flax, for it is very scarce to be had. There are some men who want to be boarded at your house, and I want you to send to me whether you are willing to board them or not. So I remain your loving wife, Elizabeth Knight."

There you see a woman of the old heroic time,—quiet, diligent, deferring to her husband, subjecting herself to the circumstances of the time, and heartily embracing the good cause. In talking of the men of the Revolution we should never forget the women, whose sacrifices were great, and whose zeal and courage in the patriot cause was abounding.

Rufus Hopkins, who seems to have been especially active and efficient in the good cause, writes Major Knight from Cranston, July 27, 1780, saying: " By express from the Governor I am requested to direct you forthwith to muster together the regiment under your command, completely equipped with arms and ammunition and six days provision ; you are therefore hereby directed accordingly, and rendezvous at Providence as soon as possible, where you are to be ready to receive further orders, the reason is said to be in consequence of Gen. Clinton's coming from New York with eight or ten thousand troops to attack the French army and fleet at Newport.'"

Scituate was not invaded, but she was called upon, and responded nobly to the call, to march her troops to the port. The British, on Sunday, Dec. 8, 1776, landed and took possession of Rhode Island, and remained there until Oct. 25, 1779, during which time the inhabitants were greatly oppressed.

In a list of Capt. Knight's company, April 20, 1775, the day after the Lexington battle, are found the following names: Joseph Knight, captain ; Samuel Wilbor, Benjamin Wood, Isaac Horton, John Hill, Nathan Walker, James Parker, John Bennet, jr., Jeremiah Abny, Joseph Remington, Nathan Ralfe, John I. Kilton, Jonathan Knight, jr., Joseph Briggs, David Knight, Joseph Collins, William Taylor, John Manchester, Edward Bennett, Thomas Parker, John Edwards, jr., Simeon Wilbor, Isaiah Austin, Samuel Eldridge, Christopher Knight, Samuel Hopkins, Benajah Bosworth, Obadiah Rolfe, Ezekiel Wood, Caleb Fisk, doctor, John Phillips, Constant Graves, Stukely Thornton, James Andrews, jr., Christopher Collins, Joseph Bennet, Thomas Knight, Peleg Colvin, Eleazor Westcott, Caleb Steere, Collins Roberts, Daniel Fisk, William Knight, Nathan Franklin, Uriah Franklin, jr., Ephriam Edwards, Stephen Edwards, Francis Fuller, jr., Benjamin Whitmore, William Stafford, Daniel Angell, Furmer Tanner—fifty-two in all.

Another list, dated Feb. 5, 1776, gives the following additional names: Daniel Dexter, Peter Pierce, Alexander Lovell, Ebenezer Handy, Joseph Turner, John Gunnison, Isaiah Ashton, Benjamin

Bacon, Nathan Mathewson, Christopher Edwards, Knight Wilbor, Abraham Angell, Moses Colvin.

An order of Capt. Knight to Aaron Fisk, one of his corporals, dated Dec. 8, 1774, directs to notify every enlisted soldier to appear in arms complete, to appear at the new dwelling-house of Lieut. Samuel Wilbor, Jan. 16, 1775.

Lieut.-Col. Ezekiel Cornell, of Col. Hitchcock's regiment, Providence, writes to Major Knight, dated Warwick, July 20, 1777, informing that he has just received an express telling him that forty sail of square-rigged vessels were off Watch Point standing towards Newport, last evening; also, desiring me to send an express to Col. Colwell, which I have done, ordering him immediately to warn the militia to be in readiness.

Return of the Scituate Light Infantry company, Benj. Boss, captain, and Richard Rhodes, clerk, gives captain and two lieutenants, one ensign, four sergeants, three corporals, four drummers and fifers, thirty-eight rank and file—total fifty-four.

The return of Capt. Nathan Worker's company gives Lieut. Joseph Carpenter, Ensign Samuel Wilbor, seventy-two men, eight all equipped, and twenty-nine guns.

Capt. Coman Smith's company had Lieut. Fabel Angell, and Capt. Herenden's company had Lieut. Isaac Hopkins, and Ensign James Wells. Timothy Hopkins, jr., was adjutant. Jos. Kimball's company had Gideon Cornwell, lieutenant. Capt. Edwin Knight's company had Ensign Daniel Baker. Capt. Herenden, Lieut. Wm. Howard, Ensign Reuben Read.

The small pox prevailed much in the army at different times, causing alarm, and the town of Scituate voted that the house of widow Mercy Angell and the house of Peleg Fiske, Esq., be opened as hospitals for the innoculation of the small pox.

Capt. Joseph Kimball, by vote of the town, Nov. 15, 1777, was appointed to supply the families of officers and soldiers, in the continental service, with the necessary articles of life, according to a late act of the General Assembly.

The returns of the Third Regiment, made to Major Knight, of

eight companies, are as follows : Capt. Potter, 75 men, Capt. Dor-
rance, 67 men, Capt. Smith, 123 men, Capt. Paine, 109 men, Capt.
Wilbour, 76 men, Capt. Howard, 64 men, Capt. Medbury, 32 men,
Capt. Rolfe, 67 men.

We get some idea of the imperfect equipments of the soldiers
in the return of three companies of two hundred and seventy-two
privates. Of these, without bayonets, one hundred and one, with
bayonets, twenty-six, and cartouches of the same number only forty-
three.

The Rhode Island soldiers in our civil war received much
praise for their brave and effective service, and their fine appearance. A Massachusetts man, writing for a newspaper, at the commencement of the rebellion, from Washington, July, 1861, says :
"Three cheers for Rhode Island rang along the avenue to-day, as
the quota of that gallant State marched proudly along, the first
battalion escorting the second, which had just been landed. Cheers
were given for the continental color carried by the second battalion
and for the ladies who marched bravely with the file-closers of two
companies, rivalling Florence Nightingale. A baggage train
brought up the rear." ' Another writer says of them : "This is
the finest and best furnished body of men in the field."

CHURCHES, SCHOOLS, MINISTERS AND PHYSICIANS.

In the history of a place there are some things more important
than its size or wealth. Its farms, manufactures, trade, are indeed
to be considered. The services performed in war, when they have
reference to the establishment of freedom, or its preservation, ought
to hold our attention :

> "By fairy hands their knell is rung,
> By forms unseen their dirge is sung:
> There Honor comes, a pilgrim grey,
> To bless the turf that wraps their clay;
> And Freedom shall awhile repair,
> To dwell, a weeping hermit, there."

Improvements in the laying out of roads, the introduction of
steam travel, the erection of public and private buildings, are not
to be forgotten, but remembered, also should be first and foremost,

Religion, as seen in the churches and families, social and business intercourse, and political institutions, and pervading the community.

The schools and higher seminaries of instruction are, with religion, to be examined as institutions lying at the foundation of a respectable, orderly, intelligent town, and household behavior, and teaching by precept and example on the part of parents, tend much to refine and elevate society.

Physicians and ministers are so placed as to healing power in body and soul, to their giving a healthy tone to society and encouraging all goodness, that their character and abilities may properly come under scrutiny. School teachers, out of school as well as in, may encourage and sustain all good works.

Religion came and followed our original settlers in this town, but they were opposed to taxation, and their ministers probably received at first only such recompense as private individuals might occasionally give them. The Friends were of this kind, and the Baptists also, and these denominations were the two earliest in the field, and probably established their religious meetings at about the same time.

Rhode Island was from the start tolerant of all protestant religious faith, allowing the freest utterance of doctrine, from which cause she attracted settlers of various creeds. Quakers and Baptists were the most numerous. The Friends, or Quakers, had a church burnt in Scituate before the Revolutionary war, showing how early they began to erect church edifices. Dec. 14, 1811, their last meeting house was erected, and William Almy and Moses Brown attended from Providence. Mr. Elihu Bowen, one of their preachers living in Scituate, wrote in his record book of the church, of the proceedings: "William being livingly opened in Gospel love to the edification of the auditory, and concluded in prayer and supplication to the Father of our mercies." Of late, owing to decline in membership of Friends, few or none are the gatherings in the town.

They, at one time, numbered in their ranks many of the most important citizens of the town. The Wilkinsons of the first generation, James Aldrich, Daniel Fiske, Isaac Fiske, Ezra Potter, John Potter, Mr. Mial Smith, Hon. Elisha Mathewson, and Gideon Harris attended the meetings.

Their first church was built on land given by Gideon Harris, a mile west of the present church building, near the old bank, and. was supposed to have been accidentally consumed. Meetings were subsequently held in private houses, sometimes with Elizabeth Aldrich, Mr. Mial Smith and Elihu Bowen, until a new house was built.

The Six Principle Baptist Church, according to a sermon of Richard Knight, one of their elders, preached in 1727, was constituted in 1725, received a grant of an acre of land and built a meeting house upon it, reserving a part of the land for a burial place. This was about the centre of the town. In August, 1827, Samuel Fiske was ordained pastor, and Benjamin Fiske, deacon of the society. The services were performed by Elders Brown, Morse and Martin. James Colvin was ordained colleague with Elder Fiske about 1738. Elder Colvin died in 1755, and the church was without a pastor until July 8, 1762, when Reuben Hopkins was ordained elder, and the church prospered under the able and useful ministry of their " nourishing pastor." A reformation commenced and continued several years, and numbers were added to the church. In 1821 they built a new and larger meeting-house on the same spot, which is still standing and in use. Elder Jaques is the present preacher and the meetings are regularly held. This church and ministry has doubtless exerted a very great and beneficial influence upon the town.

An Episcopal Church was established at Richmond village, South Scituate, several years since, having quite an extensive membership.

A meeting-house was put up in Hemlock, Foster, by the Calvinistic Baptists, but was never finished. It was bought by the town for a town house, with a provision that the house should be open for preaching. Elder John Williams was their first minister, and his colleague was Elder John Westcott. In 1827 these preachers were between eighty and ninety years of age, and still continuing their labors in the ministry, although Elder Williams preached but seldom. He addressed the convention called to ratify the constitutution, forty years before, against the measure.

The church at Foster was at first in connection with the Calvinistic Baptist Churches, but they separated about 1780, and became a Six Principle Baptist Church. Elder John Williams erected a house about 1790, at Hopkins Mills, a very elevated site.

Elder Young was the pastor of the Calvinistic Baptist Church, in Foster, and had a large family. One of his sons, Zadock, became a judge; and his son, Abiather, had some reputation as a poet.

A Congregational Church was formed at North Scituate, and organized January 1st, 1831. A house of worship was dedicated in 1834 and is now standing and occupied. Pastors: Revs. Benjamin Allen, Charles P. Grosvenor, Benjamin J. Relyea, James Hall, Charles C. Beaman, Thomas Williams, Loring P. Marsh, J. N. H. Dow, William A. Fobes, J. M. Wilkins, Thomas L. Ellis, J. H. Mellish. All now living except Allen and Ellis.

A Methodist Church is established at Richmond village, South Scituate; also, one at Ashland village, and also another at Hope village. All now in a flourishing condition.

A Free Baptist Church, having a comfortable house of worship, has long been in existence in the north-west part of the town.

In North Scituate a Free Will Baptist Church was gathered January 7th, 1832, as a branch of the Smithfield F. B. Church, with thirty-two members, Rev. Reuben Allen, pastor. Church organized April 22d, 1835, with thirty members. Pastors: Revs. Martin J. Steere, Eli Noyes, D. P. Cilley, Reuben Allen, J. B. Sargent, John Chanly, Amos Redlon, William H. Bowen, O. H. True, J. M. Brewster, L. P. Bickford. All but Allen, Noyes and Cilley now living.

SCHOOLS.

The town did not begin very early, as a corporation, to establish schools. For a long time education was left to the people to do as they pleased as to the employment of teachers. They taught in private houses, or in rooms of other buildings. Miss Fiske taught in a room of her father's tavern, seventy years ago. Marvin Morris, from Dudley, Mass., kept school for half a dozen years, about 1800 ; he was called a good penman. Thomas Mowry was a teacher, and a Mr. Dutton ; also Samuel Perry from Connecticut.

The first town appropriation recorded was $300, in 1834. This continued for successive years until 1850, when the sum advanced to $900, and so continued a number of years. It has still further advanced, and $3,000 have been voted the last two years. The town has built school houses in locations convenient for the scholars, and they are handsome structures, fitted up with recent improvements, and kept in good order. The report of the school committee for the year ending April, 1876, says, that from observation they believe that in school property they favorably compare with the most progressive towns of the State.

SMITHVILLE SEMINARY AND LAPHAM INSTITUTE,

Founded in 1839. First principal, Hosea Quimby, from 1839 to 1854 ; second principal, Samuel P. Coburn, from 1854 to 1857 ; third principal, Rev. W. Colgrove, from 1857 to 1859. Up to this time the school had been known as Smithfield Seminary. From 1859 to 1863 there was no school. In 1863 name was changed to Lapham Institute, and Rev. B. F. Hayes was principal from 1863 to 1865 ; Thomas L. Angell was principal from 1865 to 1867 ; Geo. H. Ricker was principal from 1867 to 1874 ; A. G. Moulton was principal from 1874 to 1875 ; W. S. Stockbridge was principal in 1875 and 1876.

BANK.

There has been one bank in Scituate for a long time, called the Citizens Union Bank, changed to Scituate National Bank.

PHYSICIANS.

Physicians occupy an important place in the community. In the absence of educated and settled ministers, as was the case in many parts of Rhode Island in former periods, they seem to have been the only educated class passing round in the community. Their labors must have been toilsome ; riding on horseback over the bad roads, and going great distances by night and by day.

Such men deserve to be held in grateful remembrance. They often exercise a refining and christian influence, and have done very much to prolong life. In the Revolutionary war they distinguished themselves both in the army and at home.

Dr. Ephriam Bowen, of Providence, used to ride extensively in Scituate and the adjoining towns before the conflict of the Revolution. He died about sixty years ago, aged more than ninety. Contemporary with him was Dr. Benjamin Slack who lived in the extreme north-east part of Scituate. He came from Massachusetts about 1750. The oldest record of him in Scituate is the birth of his daughter, Mary, Sept. 28, 1753. His first wife, Phœbe Slack, " the virtuous wife of Benjamin Slack, Esq.," departed this life July 8, 1762, as her grave-stone, the oldest with an inscription in the town, inform us. Dr. Slack was much esteemed, and his practice was great in Glocester, Smithfield, Scituate, and other towns. He left quite a large and good farm. His second wife was Miss Hannah Harris, of Johnston, whom he married, March 5, 1767, Gideon Harris, Esq., town clerk of Scituate, officiating at the service.

Dr. John Barden, in the north-west part of Scituate, three or four miles west of Dr. Slack, during, and after the war of the Revolution, had considerable reputation as a doctor, and used to take long rides into Massachusetts, where he had many friends and much practice.

Dr. John Wilkinson, a medical practitioner of high estimation in Scituate, was also a distinguished surgeon in the Revolutionary war.

Dr. Caleb Fiske was a man of much distinction in the town, living on Bald Hill, at the south-east part of the town. He was the son of John and Elizabeth Fiske, early settlers in the place, and was born Feb. 24, 1753. He was president of the Rhode Island Medical Society, acquired much property and left to the society $2,000, and most of the remainder to his grandson, Caleb F. Rea.

Dr. Owen Battey was in medical practice for many years, but retired in later life. He was president of the Exchange Bank, at

Greeneville, in Smithfield, and held the office of post master in South Scituate for a long time, through many party changes. He was a gentleman of the old school and highly esteemed. His father was Joshua Battey, and his grandfather, by the mother's side, was Oliver Arnold. His great-grandfather, Owen Arnold, was a British officer who came out to this country and engaged in the French war. He died July 24, 1762, in his ninetieth year.

Dr. Jeremiah Cole, who studied medicine with Dr. Anthony, of Foster, resided about a mile and a half west of North Scituate village. He was esteemed in his practice, died suddenly, May 7, 1843, in his seventy-third year, shortly after his removal to Olneyville.

Dr. Cyril Carpenter, in that part of Scituate now Foster, lived in the latter part of the last century, and from him descended two generations in the healing art : his son Thomas and his grandson, Thomas O. Carpenter, a skillful doctor of great promise, who died early.

Dr. John H. Anthony practiced medicine, residing in North Scituate for many years, but his health failing him he removed to Providence, where he died. ·

Dr. T. K. Newhall, after practicing about seventeen years in the town, removed to Providence.

Drs. James E. Roberts, Charles N. Fisher and William H. Bowen, the present physicians in Scituate, have long enjoyed the respect and confidence of our citizens.   ·

LAWYERS IN SCITUATE.

Jonah Titus was for more than forty years a resident lawyer of this town. He removed to Providence in 1865, where he died at an advanced age in May, 1876.

Charles H. Page is now a resident lawyer of Scituate, having lived here since boyhood. He has an office in Providence. Both have represented the town in both brances of the General Assembly.

HOPE FURNACE.

Hope furnace, in Scituate, for the casting of cannon, manufacture of bar iron and nails, became well known before and during the Revolutionary war. They used to cast two cannon at a time. Ore was obtained from the bed in Cranston and carted to the furnace.

In 1765, the discovery of another bed of iron in the same locality caused a company to be formed and a furnace to be erected at Hope village. Thirteen new cannon, cast at the Hope furnace, were fired at the Great Bridge, in Providence, in honor of the Declaration of Independence, July 26, 1776. Stephen Hopkins was one of the earliest and most influential of the men who got up this company, and his eldest son, Rufus, who had been a sea captain, was for many years superintendent at the furnace. Wrought iron nails were also made at Hope furnace.

MECHANICS.

Some of the mechanics in Scituate in early times were the following:

Elihu Bowen, who removed from Swanzey in 1773, was the first tanner in Scituate, having his tannery by the Moswansicut brook. He died in his eighty-eighth year, and was buried in the old Quaker burial ground. His funeral was a "large and solemn meeting."

Elihu Fiske was a good cabinet maker; Jonathan Hill learned cabinet making of him. Mr. Fiske came from Newport and became rich; keeping also, a tavern.

Capt. Thomas Hill learned his trade as a carpenter of Hugh Cole. Richard Philips learned of him also.

Daniel Smith, blacksmith, died sixty years ago.

Thomas Field's cooper shop was well known.

Mr. Angell's blacksmith shop, near the Angell tavern, was carried on by a different branch of that family from the tavern keeper, and continued in the family for several generations.

THE CORLISS ENGINE.

Our own State, "Little Rhoda," as she is called, has won the proud distinction of furnishing the steam engine whose power moves the whole machinery at the Exhibition. In other respects in

our varied and extensive manufactures on exhibition at Philadelphia
this State makes a noble contribution to American workmanship,
and receives commendations from all observers.

OBSERVATIONS.

It is with just pride that we have surveyed the past of Scituate : and let us ever honor the memory of the men and women who
have preceded us in our history, and who have bequeathed to us so
many privileges and blessings : Freedom to worship God, a free
representative government, the hope of Christianity, and the glorious anticipations of a liberty covering the whole earth with the
freedom with which CHRIST makes free, are among the rich gifts
which have come down to us from our fathers. As God was with
them, so may He be with us.

Comparing the present with past times we find our State greatly advanced in wealth and population ; and while commerce has
declined, manufactures have attained great prosperity. The old
hand looms for weaving cloth, as used in families, have given place
to the more wonderful machinery of our numerous mills, moved by
our water falls and steam engines. The spinning wheels and hand
cards are laid aside also, because of modern inventions. We cannot say as much for farming, although Americans have astonished
the world in agricultural implements ingeniously contrived to re-
lieve the farmer's toil and do the work better, and on a grander
scale. Some good farms, well managed, and made remunerative,
remain, but the larger number are still untilled, or are so much neglected that they are growing up to brush.

Facilities for education are much greater. The common
schools are superior to those of early times.

One design in the earnest and united declaration of this centennary Fourth of July is to increase the spirit of PATRIOTISM, to
arouse the nation to a deeper sense of their privileges, to revive
the memory of Our Fathers by repeating their deeds and by glow-
ing eulogiums on their valor, love of liberty, spirit of self-sacrifice
and regard for the welfare of those who should come after them.

All our revolutionary actors are in their graves—new generations have risen, new discoveries have been made, and a new aspect has come over the land. Wealth has increased, intelligence has been diffused, large cities have grown up, manufactures and the mechanic arts have flourished, our territory has lapped over to the shores of the western sea, and our name is great among the nations as a young giant arisen upon the earth.

But all this prosperity may be our ruin, and wealth and fame and luxury, and its consequent evils, may prove a false dependence.

> " What constitutes a State ?
> Not high raised battlement or labored mound,
>   Thick wall, or moated gate ;
> Not cities proud, with spires and turrets crowned ;
>   Not bays and broad-armed ports,
> Where, laughing at the storm, rich navies ride ;
>   Not starred and spangled courts,
> Where low-born baseness wafts perfume to pride ;
>   No—men, high-minded men ;
>
> " Men who their duties know,
> But know their rights, and knowing dare maintain :
>   These constitute a State."

A nation wholly intent upon sordid gain, given up to frivolous pleasures, separate from God and holiness, forgetful of the fathers, from whom, under God, they received their blessings, is necessarily a weak and pusillanimous nation, as the history of Rome and other similar empires proves. If to these declensions are to be added, dishonesty of bankers and men in trade, corruption of men in public life, to the extent of making dishonest gain the usual concomitant of an office-holder and legislator, and bribery at the voting place, carried on without a blush, quite a practice, and increasingly more so, why, then there is pressing need of an awakening of the people to make the inquiry, " Whither are we drifting ? " At such a juncture of affairs, as believed in by many of the more thoughtful and deserving, as coming upon us as a people this present celebration, recalling vividly to mind the more simple and honest days of the Republic, and holding up for emulation the characters of the period of 1776, when persons were put into the crucible and tried, as it were, by fire, and came out pure gold, for all countries and ages to admire, and when Washington took his place as in the heavens a shining star for all time—a sight of all this—the entering of it, as it were, into the very souls of the people, and taking possession of them, may well be held as the sacred duty of all who are privileged to be the orators of the hour.

Before us lies a new century, on which the nation is about to enter. Great as were the perils supposed to be incident to the first, they have been gallantly met, by the several generations, and overcome. God's hand, clearly seen in colonial times, was still more visible in the national history which followed, and to Him we must look for guidance and blessing. Very timely is the President's proclamation, and very proper and well expressed. Great would have been the oversight if it had been forgotten. It says:

" The founders of the government, at its birth and in its feebleness, invoked the blessings and protection of a Divine Providence, and the thirteen colonies and three millions of people have expanded into a nation of strength and numbers, commanding the position which then was demanded, and for which fervent prayers were then offered. It seems fitting that on the occurrence of the hundredth anniversary of our existence as a nation, a grateful acknowledgment should be made to Almighty God for the protection and bounties which He has vouchsafed to our beloved country, and humbly to invoke a continuance of His favor and of His protection."

We trust there will be a two-century life of our nation; that we may continue united, prosperous and free up to that period, but none of us will be alive to witness it. The imagination toils in vain to picture the two-century spectacle. A hundred years more must make many changes, but what they will be no one can tell. We must pass through several generations, who will in turn come to preside, as the administration and the people. More territory may be added, and more people and more wealth acquired, and new discoveries make as great changes in the future as the steam engine and the telegraph have wrought in the past.

Civil war, a contest between the North and South, was what Washington feared, and warned the people of both sections against those who should attempt to put variances between them. But his farewell address was disregarded by both sides, and the result of civil war, naturally, and as it were, inevitably followed. Contests may arise in the future, but it will not come on the subject of slavery. It is with profound satisfaction that we to-day can look around and exclaim: "No slave breathes the air of our country." Never again will that stain make an American ashamed of his nationality.

We must cultivate love and forbearance with one another; and especially we should, in our centennial, reach our hands over the bloody chasm and cultivate friendly relations with the South, since the rebellion has been put down and the people have submitted to the result. To-day they, with us, unite in a centennial, which is theirs as well as ours. North and South participated in the battles of the Revolution, and the South and the North unite in the rejoicings over the glory of our common heritage.

The East may feel a little sensitive at the waning of their political supremacy, and the West may not a little exult that they are rising in the scale of comparative greatness, but let us bear in mind that the East has sent her children West, and that the greatness of the West is the theme of our own glory.

The shores of the Pacific and the Atlantic may engender suspicions of the unjust political favors awarded to one more than the other, but mutual concessions and kindnesses, and the rapid growth of California and Oregon will naturally, and without opposition, bring to these territories increased and increasing influence. Let us be just to all sections, and we need not fear any hostility tending to disunion.

The great cry of the day is for retrenchment and economy in public and private expenditures. Honest men and able should be sought after for office, and both of the great political parties should have their proportionate share of public offices, and thus a civil service reform will be created which every patriot should encourage.

Two great political parties should always exist, and they should be nearly equal in numbers, power and influence, that they may watch each other and correct any mistakes or frauds that may be discovered. Ceaseless watchfulness of our rulers and their doings is the price the people must pay for the blessings of liberty!

The people, and the people only, in the teachings of history, **can** be safely trusted to preserve and hand down freedom.

In the words of our poet Longfellow, apostrophizing our country, as a ship sailing on the ocean, we may hopefully say:

> " Thou too sail on, O ship of State!
> Sail on, O Union strong and great!
> Humanity, with all its fears,
> With all the hopes of future years,
> Is hanging breathless on thy fate!
> We know what master laid thy keel,
> What workmen wrought thy ribs of steel,
> Who made each mast, and sail, and rope,
> What anvils rung, what hammers beat,
> In what a forge and what a heat
> Were shaped the anchors of thy hope!
> Fear not each sudden sound and shock—
> 'Tis of the wave, and not the rock;
> 'Tis but the flapping of the sail,
> And not a rent made by the gale.
> In spite of rock, and tempest's roar,
> In spite of false lights on the shore,
> Sail on, nor fear to breast the sea!
> Our hearts, our hopes, our prayers, our tears,
> Our faith triumphant o'er our fears,
> Are all with thee,—are all with thee! "

Let the day be given to patriotic and grateful recollections of the honored dead; the men and women who braved the perils of the sea and the wilderness, and built their homes for wives and little ones, where wild and ferocious beasts of prey and savage men roamed the forests.

Sacred to the memory, also, of those whose love of liberty impelled them, at all hazards, to enter a solemn protest against the entrance of every form of tyranny and unjust edicts, and to resist with all their might, even unto death, the armed forces sent out by Great Britain to subjugate the people.

A careful enquiry would show the nobleness of mind and patriotic devotion of the *women* of the Revolutionary period, who not only made no opposition, and uttered no complaint, but cheered the men, who were compelled to leave, hardly begun, the clearing of the wilderness, and the care and protection of their young families, to rush to the camp and the battle field, and lay down their lives, if need be, that their children and their children's children might not come under the burdens of unjust and tyrannical governments to which the world had been so long subject, and might possess the free representative government, which we now enjoy.

Shame would it be!—if there were not a spontaneous and universal uprising all over our land, to proclaim to the world that the sins of ingratitude and forgetfulness of our benefactors, the heroes of the Revolution, and of all who since that period have, in office and out of office, and of all political parties, who have aided in carrying out in continued practice the principles and spirit of 1776 until now, one hundred years from the memorable Declaration, our liberties have been preserved and the threatened description of our Union averted.

Let the present generation preserve and hand down these liberties to those who may come after us; and watch with zealous care all tendencies of our nation to encroach upon the freedom our fathers won for us.

And let the sons and daughters of Rhode Island, here, within our borders, and abroad, wherever they may be scattered, bear gratefully in mind the intense love of freedom and hatred of wrong and oppression, that characterized the settlers of the State, and has ever since marked its inhabitants. Let the names of Angell, West, Knight, Williams, Aldrich, Westcott, Harris, Whipple, Green, Ellery, Perry, Hopkins, Ward, Greene, and other patriots be sounded, and with them the statesmen and heroes of all the other States,—Samuel Adams, James Otis, Putnam, Knox, Lee, and a multitude beside. Sound high and feelingly the name of LAFAYETTE, and remember gratefully the French nation.

The war of 1812-15, and the terrible civil war of 1861-4, added greatly to the number of these illustrious names that have adorned our country's annals, and laid down their lives willingly, that the glorious Union might be preserved, in the most deadly warfare ever waged to destroy it. Rhode Island, as distinguised for promptness, bravery and gallant exploits in that war, as in previous contests, hands down her names to our admiring and grateful remembrance, to the present and all coming time. Her officers and soldiers and seaman are enrolled on the undying scroll of our country's glory, and so of other States—praise, honor, thanks, we give to all.

One great name, that of the " FATHER OF HIS COUNTRY," will be everywhere sounded to-day ; and no poem, oration, song or melody shall be able to reach the height of his deserved praise, or add a single leaf to the wreath of his world-sounded renown.

His fame, now after the lapse of three-quarters of a century since his death, has suffered no diminution; his star still blazes single and alone in brightness and glory in the firmament of American Freedom ! Raised up by the Great Dispenser of Events in a critical period of the world's history, and in the birth-day of the nation destined to pour back a reflective light upon the old world, and to exert an influence in human affairs beyond that of any empire in the world's history, the American people hailed him as Moses was saluted by the Israelites when he led them out of Egypt.

It is the great glory of America that she has produced a WASHINGTON, and it will not be presumption to say that, with all our exhibitions to-day, in our centennial, we have nothing greater to ask the world's attention than to him.

APPENDIX.

DEPUTIES, SENATORS, REPRESENTATIVES, ETC.

DEPUTIES.

1731.
Joseph Wilkinson,
Stephen Hopkins,
Zachariah Rhodes.

1732.
Stephen Hopkins,
Zachariah Rhodes.

1733.
Capt. Thomas Angell,
Stephen Hopkins.

1734.
Edward Sheldon,
Capt. Thomas Angell.

1735.
Stephen Hopkins,
Benjamin Fiske.

1736.
Stephen Hopkins,
Job Randall.

1737.
Stephen Hopkins,
Thomas Realph.

1738.
Edward Sheldon,
Stephen Hopkins.

1739.
Job Randall,
James Colvin.

1740.
Job Randall,
James Colvin.

1741.
Job Randall,
Stephen Hopkins.

1742.
Job Randall,
Thomas Realph.

1743.
Capt. Job Randall,
Joseph Knight.

1744.
Capt. Job Randall,
Jeremiah Angell.

1745.
Capt. Job Randall,
Ezekiel Hopkins.

1746.
Capt. Job Randall,
Charles Harris.

1747.
Capt. Job Randall,
John Fisk.

1748.
Capt. Job Randall,
Charles Harris.

1749.
Thomas Ralph,
Thomas Hudson.

1750.
Job Randall,
Gideon Hammond.

1751.
Capt. Job Randall,
Charles Harris.
1752.
Capt. Job Randall,
Charles Harris.
1753.
Job Randall,
Capt. Thomas Relf.
1754.
Job Randall,
Capt. Amos Hammond.
1755.
Capt. Job Randall,
Capt. Amos Hammond.
1756.
Capt. Job Randall,
Gideon Harris.
1757.
Capt. Job Randall,
Jeremiah Angell.
1758.
Capt. Job Randall,
Jeremiah Angell.
1759.
Capt. Job Randall,
Jeremiah Angell.
1760.
Capt. Job Randall,
William West.
1761.
Capt. Job Randall,
William West.
1762.
Job Randall,
Jeremiah Angell.
1763.
Job Randall,
Charles Harris.
1764.
Job Randall,
Jeremiah Angell.
1765.
Job Randall,
Jeremiah Angell.
1766.
Charles Harris,
William West.
1767.
Charles Harris,
John Fiske.

1768.
Gideon Harris,
William West.
1769.
Job Randall,
Benjamin Slack.
1770.
Job Randall,
Benjamin Slack.
1771.
William West,
Charles Harris.
1772.
Ezekiel Cornell,
Rufus Hopkins.
1773.
William West,
Rufus Hopkins.
1774.
Ezekiel Cornell,
Rufus Hopkins.
1775.
Ezekiel Cornell,
Rufus Hopkins.
1776.
Col. William West,
Christopher Potter.
1777.
Job Randall, Esq.,
Timothy Hopkins, Esq.
1778.
Timothy Hopkins, Esq.,
Christopher Potter.
1779.
William West, Esq.,
Christopher Potter.
1780.
Christopher Potter,
John Williams.
1781.
William Rhodes, Esq.,
Rufus Hopkins, Esq.
1782.
William Rhodes, Esq.,
Rufus Hopkins, Esq.
1783.
William Rhodes, Esq.,
Rufus Hopkins, Esq.
1784.
Rufus Hopkins, Esq.,
William West, Esq.

APPENDIX. **3**

1785.
Rufus Hopkins, Esq.,
William West, Esq.
1786.
Nathan Bates,
Thomas Mowry, Esq.
1787.
Nathan Bates,
Thomas Mowry, Esq.
1788.
Peleg Fiske, Esq.,
James Aldrich.

1789.
Peleg Fiske, Esq.,
James Aldrich, Esq.
1790.
James Aldrich, Esq.,
Nathaniel Medbury. Esq.
1791.
... .
....
1792.
James Aldrich, Esq.,
Nathaniel Medbury, Esq.   .

REPRESENTATIVES.

1792 to 1794—February Session,
James Aldrich,
Nathaniel Medbury.
1794 to 1800—May Session,
James Aldrich,
Job Randall.
1800 to 1805—May Session,
James Aldrich,
Elisha Mathewson.
1805 to 1808—June Session,
Job Randall.
Elisha Mathewson.
1808—February Session,
Job Randall,
Peleg Fisk, jr.
1808 to 1810—May Session,
Peleg Fisk, jr.,
Charles Angell.
1810—May Session,
Charles Angell,
Solomon Taylor.
1810—June Session,
James Aldrich,
Solomon Taylor.
1811 to 1813—May Session,
Solomon Taylor,
Clements Smith.
1813—May Session.
Charles Angell.
1813—June Session,
Clements Smith.
1813—October Session,
Clements Smith,
Samuel Graves.

1814—October Session,
Elisha Mathewson,
Samuel Graves.
1815—May Session,
Elisha Mathewson,
Eleazer Relph.
1816 to 1818—May Session,
Josiah Westcott,
Isaac Field.
1818—May Session.
Josiah Westcott,
Israel Brayton.
1818 to 1820—June Session,
Elisha Mathewson,
Israel Brayton.
1820—May Session,
Elisha Mathewson,
Israel G. Manchester.
1821—May Session,
ElishaMathewson, chosen Speaker
Israel Brayton.
1821—October Session,
Jerry A. Fenner,
Israel Brayton.
1822—May Session,
ElishaMathewson,chosen Speaker
Israel Brayton.
1822—October Session,
Eleazer Relph,
....
1823—January Session,
Eleazer Relph,
Thomas Henry.

1823—October Session,
Stephen Corp,
Thomas Henry.
1824 to 1826—October Session,
Thomas Henry,
Israel Brayton.
1826—May Session,
Israel Brayton,
William Smith.
1826 to 1829—October Session,
William Smith,
Nathan K. Stone.
1829—May Session,
William Smith,
Benjamin Wilbur.
1830—May Session,
William Smith,
Job Randall.
1831 to 1833—May Session,
Benjamin Wilbur,
Job Randall.
1833—May Session,
Elisha Mathewson,
Josiah Westcott.
1833 to 1835—June Session,
Elisha Mathewson,
Jonah Titus.

1835 to 1837—October Session,
Jonah Titus,
John Aldrich.
1837—May Session,
Jonah Titus,
Wilmarth N. Aldrich.
1837 to 1841—October Session,
Elisha Mathewson,
Wilmarth N. Aldrich.
1841—May Session,
Elisha Mathewson,
Josiah Westcott.
1842—May Session,
Elisha Mathewson, Senator,
Josiah Westcott, Representative,
Andrew A. Angell,   "
1842—June Session,
Elisha Mathewson, Senator,
Job Randall, Representative,
Andrew A. Angell,   "
1843—June Session,
Job Randall, Senator,
Andrew A. Angell, Representative
Richard M. Andrew,   "
Israel Brayton,   "

SENATORS AND REPRESENTATIVES.

SENATORS.

May, 1843,
Job Randall,
May, 1844,
Job Randall,
May, 1845,
Pardon Angell,
May, 1846,
Pardon Angell,
June, 1846,
Pardon Angell,
October, 1846,
Pardon Angell,
January, 1847,
Pardon Angell,
May, 1847,
William B. Kimball,
May, 1848,
Albert Hubbard.

1849.
Josiah Wescott.
1850.
Josiah Wescott.
1851.
Pardon Angell.
1852.
Pardon Angell.
1853.
Ira Cowee.
1854.
Ira Cowee.
1855.
Isaac Saunders.
1856.
Ira Cowee.
1857.
Henry W Emmons.

1858.
Henry W. Emmons.
1859.
Henry W. Emmons.
1860.
Abner W. Peckham.
1861.
Abner W. Peckham.
1862.
Abner W. Peckham.
1863.
Abner W. Peckham.
1864.
Abner W. Peckham.
1865.
Alanson Steere.
1866.
Alanson Steere.
1867.
Alanson Steere.

1868.
Alanson Steere.
1869.
Charles H. Fisher.
1870.
John H. Barden.
1871.
John H. Barden.
1872.
Isaac Saunders.
1873.
Isaac Saunders.
1874.
Charles H. Page.
1875.
Charles H. Page.
1876.
Jeremiah H. Field.

REPRESENTATIVES.

May, 1843,
Andrew A. Angell,
Richard M. Andrew,
Israel Brayton.
May, 1844,
Richard M. Andrew,
Isreal Brayton,
Stephen H. Fiske.
May, 1845,
Wilmarth N. Aldrich,
Harley Luther,
William A. Roberts.
May, 1846,
Wilmarth N. Aldrich,
Harley Luther,
William A. Roberts.
June, 1846,
Wilmarth N. Aldrich,
Harley Luther,
Abel Salisbury.
October, 1846,
Isaac Saunders,
Harley Luther,
Abel Salisbury.
January, 1847,
Isaac Saunders,
Harley Luther,
William Roberts

May, 1847,
Albert Hubbard,
John Potter, 2d,
George Aldrich.
May, 1848,
Horace S. Patterson,
Arthur F. Aldrich,
George Aldrich.
1849.
Isaac Saunders,
Benedict Lapham.
1850.
Isaac Saunders,
Benedict Lapham,
Richard M. Andrew.
1851.
William A. Roberts,
Sheldon Fiske.
1852.
Harley P. Angell,
William A. Roberts.
1853.
Jonah Titus,
Albert K. Barnes.
1854.
Jonah Titus.
Albert K. Barnes.

1855.
Arthur F. Randall,
Henry Hierliby.
1856.
Charles Jackson,
Pardon A. Phillips.
1857.
Andrew A. Angell,
Isaac Saunders.
1858.
Andrew A. Angell,
Isaac Saunders.
1859.
Andrew A. Angell,
Samuel P. Boss.
1860.
Welcome Matteson,
Henry S. Olney.
1861.
Welcome Matteson,
Henry S. Olney.
1862.
Albert W. Harris,
Henry A. Lawton.
1863.
Olney H. Austin,
John S. Fiske.
1864.
Olney H. Austin,
John S. Fiske.
1865.
Samuel G. Allen,
William G. Smith.

1866.
William G. Smith,
Andrew J. Wescott.
1867.
Martin Smith,
Andrew J. Wescott.
1868.
Martin Smith,
Henry A. Lawton.
1869.
John H. Barden,
Ferdinand H. Allen.
1870.
Hiram Steere,
Richard G. Howland.
1871.
Hiram Steere,
Isaac Saunders.
1872.
Charles H. Page,
Harris H. Stone.
1873.
Charles H. Page.

1874.
Martin S. Smith.

1875.
Martin S. Smith.

1876.
Benjamin Wilbour.

MODERATORS OF TOWN MEETINGS.

Stephen Hopkins, 1730.
Capt. Joseph Brown, 1731.
Benjamin Fisk, 1732.
Stephen Hopkins, 1733.
Benjamin Fisk, 1734.
Edward Sheldon, 1735.
Stephen Hopkins, 1737.
Job Randall, 1739.
James Brown, 1746.
Benjamin Fisk, 1742.
Capt. Charles Harris, 1747.
Job Randall, 1759.

William West, 1765.
Charles Harris, 1765.
William West, 1765.
Charles Harris, 1766.
John Fisk, 1768.
Ezekiel Cornell, 1768.
Rufus Hopkins, 1778.
Reuben Hopkins, 1779.
Benjamin Slack, 1780.
Rufus Hopkins, 1780.
Benjamin Slack, 1781.
Timothy Hopkins, 1781.

Ezekiel Cornell, 1781.
Dr. Caleb Fisk, 1781.
Benjamin Slack, 1781.
Rufus Hopkins, 1781.
Caleb Fisk, 1783.
Ezekiel Cornell, 1785.
Rufus Hopkins, 1786.
Reuben Hopkins, 1787.
Col. Clemons Smith, 1825.
Jonah Titus, 1826.
Clemons Smith, 1827.
Jonah Titus, 1828.
Clemons Smith, 1829.
Elisha Mathewson, 1831.
Jonah Titus, 1832.
Jerry A. Fenner, 1832.
Elisha Mathewson, 1833.
Jonah Titus, 1834.
Elisha Mathewson, 1834.
Benjamin Wilbur, 1835.
Flavel Patterson, 1835.
Olney Battey, 1836.
John Graves, 1837.
Israel Brayton, 1838.
Owen Battey, 1838.
Israel Brayton, 1839.

Flavel Patterson, 1839.
Jonah Titus, 1840.
Elisha Mathewson, 1840.
David Phillips, 3d, 1841.
Isaac Saunders, 1842.
Horace Battey, 1842.
Wilmarth N. Aldrich, 1845.
Jonah Titus, 1846.
Isaac Saunders, 1847.
Horace S. Patterson, 1848.
Isaac Saunders, 1849.
H. S. Patterson, 1852.
George W. Colwell, 1853.
John H. Barden, 1855.
Caleb W. Johnston, 1856.
William G. Smith, 1857.
Uriah R. Colwell, 1859.
Harley P. Angell, 1865.
Jeremiah H. Field, 1866.
Dexter A. Potter, 1867.
H. S. Patterson, 1869.
Alanson Steere, 1870.
H. S. Patterson, 1871.
Benjamin T. Albro, 1872.
William G. Smith, 1874.
Richmond M. Knight, 1876.

TOWN CLERKS.

Joseph Brown, 1730.
Stephen Hopkins, 1732.
Gideon Harris, 1741.
John Harris, 1778.
John Westcott, 1779.
John Harris, 1780.
John Westcott, pro. tem, 1809.
Josiah Westcott, 1814.
John A. Harris, 1845.
Sylvester Patterson, 1854.

Albert Hubbard, 1855.
S. Patterson, 1856.
A. Hubbard, 1857.
Isaac Saunders, pro. tem, 1861.
S. Patterson, 1861.
A. Hubbard, 1865.
S. Patterson, pro. tem, Dec. 1867
S. Patterson, 1868.
D. C. Remington, 1875.

TOWN TREASURERS.

Lieut. Joseph Wilkinson, 1730.
Joseph Wilkinson, 1731.
Benjamin Fisk, 1732.

Job Randall, 1736.
Capt. Job Randall, 1737.
Timothy Hopkins, 1758.

Jeremiah Angell, 1760.
Jonathan Hopkins, 1779.
Jonathan Hopkins, jr., 1780.
Josiah Kimball, 1781.
Joshua Smith, 1825.
Albert G. Field, 1850.
Joshua Smith, 1851.
John B. Smith, 1852.

John A. Harris, 1857.
Alpheus Winsor, 1858.
John B. Smith, 1860.
Jeremiah H. Field, 1866.
John B. Smith, 1870.
Jeremiah H. Field, 1871.
David Capwell, 1873.
Albert Hubbard, 1874.

www.ingramcontent.com/pod-product-compliance
Lightning Source LLC
Chambersburg PA
CBHW022017080426
42733CB00007B/628